PRAY
WITH THE **BIBLE**

MEDITATE
WITH THE **WORD**

The Exciting World of *Lectio Divina*

Author: Rev. Fr. Gabriel Mestre
Consultant: Ricardo Grzona, FRP, Ph.D.
Editor: Mario J. Paredes

 AMERICAN BIBLE SOCIETY

Pray with the Bible, Meditate with the Word: The Exciting World of the *Lectio Divina* has been granted the *Nihil Obstat* by Monsignor Michael F. Hull and the *Imprimatur* by +Bishop Dennis J. Sullivan. The *Nihil Obstat* and the *Imprimatur* are official declarations that this book is free of doctrinal or moral error. No implications contained therein that those who have granted the *Nihil Obstat* and *Imprimatur* agree with the content, opinion or statements expressed.

Library of Congress Control Number: 2010925921
ISBN Number: 978-1-58516-945-0
ABS Item Number: 122590

All Bible references are taken from the *Good News Translation* © 1992, American Bible Society. The *Good News Translation* was granted the *Imprimatur* by the Most Reverend Archbishop +William H. Keeler, D.D., President, National Conference of Catholic Bishops, March 10, 1993.

Illustrations on pages 35, 42, 43, 64, 65, 80, 81, 88 and 93 are used with permission of Swiss artist and storyteller, Annie Vallotton, ABS is an Interconfessional Organization and this artist comes to us from a Protestant Tradition.

For over 190 years, American Bible Society has been providing churches of all Christian faith traditions with Bibles and the Scripture resources they need to enlighten, inspire and enrich the lives of the people they serve. ABS is pleased to provide this manual on *Lectio Divina* in partnership with the Roman Catholic Church and trusts that Catholic readers will find it useful in forming and deepening their habit of meaningful Scripture reading.

American Bible Society is an interconfessional Christian organization whose mission, in part, is to work with churches and Christian organizations to make the Bible available so all people may experience its life-changing message. The specifically Catholic doctrinal positions presented in this manual do not reflect the interconfessional stance of American Bible Society.

TABLE OF CONTENTS

CHAPTER 3

CHAPTER 4

CHAPTER 5

CHAPTER 6

CONCLUSION

Easter Season 2010

My dear friends in Christ,

We live in a world that presents ever increasing demands on our time and attention. It is not unusual these days that a person is having a telephone conversation and searching the internet, both by way of a hand held electronic device, while walking down the street. In the midst of so much communication and so many distractions, it is of great importance that we allow time for prayer and reflection. Our Lord is always inviting us to draw closer and come to know Him better, but we need to accept that invitation.

Throughout the course of history, God has spoken to humanity through Sacred Scripture. Since time immemorial, men and women have come to a better understanding of God's plan for the world and for their own lives through prayer and study of the Old Testament, the Gospels, and books and letters of the New Testament. The inspired words of the Bible provide us strength in moments of challenge and guidance for living a good and holy life.

The Bible can also be a source of significant insight and wisdom if we pray with the Word of God. Through this meditation, *"Lectio Divina"*, the Lord speaks to our heart and helps us to see with the eyes of faith. This practice is not a "quick read"; we must turn off the telephones and computers, and turn toward our God. If we wish to enter into the deep friendship with Jesus, we must make the time and space to be fully aware of His presence and hear His words.

We are blessed that The American Bible Society provides us these important workshops in *Lectio Divina*. The Society is truly doing the work of the Lord, and I am most grateful for that service. The manual presented to you today will help you experience a powerful new relationship Jesus, the Eternal Word of the Father and to be His witness throughout your life.

With the assurance of my prayers for you and for those whom you hold dear, I am,

Sincerely yours in Christ,

+ Seán, OFMCap

Archbishop of Boston

LECTIO DIVINA FOR THE ROAD. . .

The reading of Scripture by the laity is no longer taboo, nor is it reserved for the intellectual elite and those consecrated to the Church. Today, in a slow but sure manner, we are assuming and experimenting with the central place to which Holy Scripture belongs in the life of the believer and the life of the Christian community.

Holy Scripture (the saving revelation and communication from God to humankind) is the fountain from which the content of our Christian life flows; and, because of that, from it also flows the full sense of our personal and common life following Christ who is "the way, the truth and the life" (John 14.6).

Our answer to the saving and revealing work of God is offered through prayer. This entails, in the first place, a true, daily and permanent consciousness of the creative and re-creative presence of God in the cosmos, in the individual, and in all humankind. This results in a lifestyle – the lifestyle of sons and daughters of God – a lifestyle that corresponds to the loving presence and communication of God, our compassionate and merciful Father, as revealed in Christ.

Lectio Divina, "the reading of the sacred" or "the divine reading" is an ancient method of the Church that dates back to the way the early Church Fathers taught the reading of the Bible. It refers specifically to the prayerful manner in which medieval monastics committed themselves to a reflective, receptive and contemplative reading of the Word of God. With the passing of time, this practice fell by the wayside. Today, thanks to the encouragement given to all the faithful by Vatican II to be regular readers of Holy Scripture as a centerpiece of the Christian life, for liturgical action and all theological reflection, Christians are once again using the methodology of *Lectio Divina*.

Lectio Divina is a method for the prayerful reading of the Holy Scriptures, but it is also a biblical movement. It is a prayerful and contemplative movement among Christians who want to return to the first fountain of the faith and find in it the true origin, identity, vision, experience and mission of Scripture. Meditation upon Holy Scripture is perhaps all the more important today given the constant distractions from everything spiritual that result in the restlessness and anxiety that is so common in our society. Only the Scriptures can satisfy the insatiable thirst among men and women looking for the true sense of the eternal God, infinite and transcendent.

At this historic juncture as we transition from the modern to the post-modern, people of all walks of life, races and beliefs, and especially people in our great cities, experience the need for space, time and methods which allow for and facilitate an encounter with the divine, the eternal, the Absolute. And because science and technology has not been able to solve the overwhelming problems of humanity such as hunger, war, inequities, injustices, the thousand forms of violence, division, hatred, etc., there is a greater longing for the answers to come from the spiritual arena.

Therefore, *Lectio Divina* is presented as a method which encourages and makes possible an encounter with God, with his revelation, his communication, his Word, his saving plan, his intention, his will, his way. It is a method whose time has returned and needs to be promoted for use among individuals, small Christian communities such as families and "home churches," ecclesiastic communities such as prayer groups and parishes. In all these situations we can experience anew the Kingdom of God in our midst, the first fruits of salvation, a foretaste of heaven on earth.

American Bible Society, an inter-confessional Christian organization that translates, publishes and distributes the Bible ". . . so that all may experience its life changing message," promotes and encourages *Lectio Divina* so that the Word of God will be better known, loved, practiced and lived by men and women of good will.

We are pleased with the spiritual transformation that this Bible reading method can bring to our personal lives in the bosom of our communities and Christian Churches. We also desire that *Lectio Divina* will make of us better human beings and better Christians, dedicated to the construction of a better world: more just, more fraternal, more humane and more divine.

Mario J. Paredes
American Bible Society
Presidential Liaison Catholic Ministries

FOREWORD

Today the term *Lectio Divina* is becoming increasingly well known in the Catholic Church. A few years ago this was not the case. This ancient system of praying and meditating upon the Scriptures was once almost exclusively reserved for monasteries where it was used by monks. It found some adherents in a few seminaries where those preparing for the ordained ministry used these exercises for the prayerful reading of Sacred Scriptures. Priests who studied in those seminaries in years past tell us that biblical studies were not common.

When Pope John Paul XXIII convoked the Second Vatican Council, among the many subjects discussed, Holy Scripture was given a place of prominence. In fact, one of the most important documents that came out of the Council was *Dei Verbum*, *Word of God*.

As a result, our generation enjoys the availability of the complete Bible in our principal languages and many in the world have access to the Bible in their homes. Centuries ago, there were only hand-written copies, available for use during liturgies and for study in monasteries. The invention of the printing press did not immediately change much as most people were still illiterate. The Reformation caused the Catholic Church to preserve and reinforce the Sacred Scriptures, especially in the liturgy. Following the Second Vatican Council, Catholic Christians have been making dynamic headway, and the younger generations are excited about the Bible when it is presented to them in their own language.

The present manual will give us the opportunity to be concrete and enable us to understand the Bible as the written Word of God with its meaning for us today. The ancient and traditional method of *Lectio Divina* will enlighten our understanding and lead us into a living relationship with the Good News.

Having participated in great events of the Catholic Church such as the Congress that celebrated the fortieth anniversary of *Dei Verbum*, and serving as auditor for the Synod of the Word, I can say with all certainty that those who experience spiritual renewal in the Church owe that revival to the prayerful reading of Sacred Scripture.

May Jesus Christ, the Eternal Word whom the Father gave to redeem us, enrich our lives everyday through the constant and disciplined exercise of *Lectio Divina*.

Brother Ricardo Grzona, FRP, Ph.D.
President Ramon Pane Foundation
Miami

INTRODUCTION

The central theme of the document at hand is the prayerful reading of the Bible. Thanks be to God for the increase in printed and digital documents that help us understand *Lectio Divina*.

This manual opens with a brief outline and general introduction of Sacred Scripture. The first four chapters constitute an introduction to *Lectio Divina*. The significance of the Bible, its origin and the content, our understanding of Scripture, the Bible-Church relationship, and the understanding of the mystery of Christ in the Sacred Texts, are a few themes discussed in the first three chapters. Chapter four explains the "spirituality of the Word" in our pursuit of Christ. The Lord is the center of all Scripture. He is the living Word who invites every human being to follow him with a sincere desire to live out the gospel.

Chapter five is dedicated to the history and the efforts to define the prayerful reading of the Bible. It also reviews the rich Papal and Magisterial reflections following the Second Vatican Council on *Lectio Divina*. Chapter six gives a detailed description of the traditional steps of *Lectio Divina*. Finally, in the conclusion two practical exercises for prayerful reading of the Bible are included. These will be very helpful for a comparative study of the *Lectio Divina* method.

This is a simple manual that will be beneficial for under-standing the prayerful reading of the Scripture within the framework of the Church. We hope that it will be useful to both individuals and communities that desire to sincerely dedicate themselves to the exciting world of the prayerful reading of the Bible.

May God make the reading of these pages encouraging for all who desire to place their hope in the Lord and in his Word. May the Word of God enlighten our path of life. With the psalmist we can say: **"I am worn out, Lord, waiting for you to save me; I place my trust in your word."** (Psalm 119.81) and **"Your word is a lamp to guide me and a light for my path"** (Psalm 119.105).

CHAPTER 1

DELVING INTO THE MYSTERY OF THE BIBLE

INTRODUCTION

The Bible, Scripture, the Book, Sacred Text, Sacred Scripture, Holy Books and Holy Bible are some of the terms used to refer to the very special "book" which we commonly call the Bible, and which Christians of diverse confessions use as their guide for life and spirituality.

HOW CAN WE DEFINE THE BIBLE?

The term Bible comes from the Greek word *biblos*, which literally means "books." The Bible truly is a book and, at the same time, a collection of books. It contains a group of books that were written over a long period of time and in a variety of cultural contexts. The Vatican Council tells us:

> Sacred Scripture is the word of God inasmuch as it is consigned to writing
> under the inspiration of the divine Spirit.[1]

This phrase defines the essential nature of the Bible: it is the written Word of God. In October 2009, the Church convened the Synod of Bishops where "the Word of God in the Life and Mission of the Church" was the theme. At the Synod, in the final message, the Fathers gave a dynamic definition of the Bible:

> *The Sacred Scriptures "bear witness" to the divine word in written form.*
> *They memorialize the creative and saving event of revelation by way of*
> *canonical, historical and literary means.* [2]

This definition, while maintaining the essential element of what *Dei Verbum* is, identifies the Word as "the creative and saving revelation" of God. We can thus say that the Bible is the written experience of God's revelation, through his love for humankind and our response to that divine love. It is the history of human understanding of God's revelation and the pursuit of a better way of life. God gives himself to his people, and trusting in him guarantees a full life. This profound experience of encounter is comprehended in the "canonical, historical and literary memorial" that we call Sacred Scripture.

The Bible is divided into two sections: the Old Testament and the New Testament.

The first section, known as the **Old Testament** contains 46 books that include, among other things, the following themes and topics:

- God's revelation through his creation of the world and the creation of human beings in his own image and likeness.
- Human beings are the crown of God's creative work, and are called to lead the entire cosmos.
- Human beings did not always respond to God's plan with love; instead, they turned away from him, sinning and facing the consequence of death.
- God did not abandon his creation; he renewed his love and formed an alliance with a people and through them, he brought humanity to salvation.
- Humanity continued to succumb to temptation by turning its back on God, yet God kept his covenant and eternal promise of salvation.

The second section of the Bible we call the **New Testament**. It contains 27 books and it narrates:

- The events that are central to our faith: the birth, death, resurrection and ascension of our Lord Jesus Christ, who is truly God and truly man.
- The fulfillment of God's definitive covenant through Christ, the redemption of humanity and granting of life in its fullness.
- The establishment of a new people, the Church, who are called to bear witness to God's message of life to the entire world.

The following descriptions define Sacred Scripture:

- The written Word of God is the narration of God's revelation through the creation of the world.
- This Word of God is firm, effective and permanent.

"Yes, grass withers and flowers fade, but the word of our God endures forever" (Isaiah 40.8).

"Heaven and earth will pass away, but my words will never pass away" (Mark 13.31).

"The word of God is alive and active, sharper than any double-edged sword. It cuts all the way through, to where soul and spirit meet, to where joints and marrow come together. It judges the desires and thoughts of the heart" (Hebrews 4.12).

THE WORD OF GOD IN HUMAN LANGUAGE

The Bible is God's written Word. It is also the effort of many individuals inspired by the Holy Spirit. The Second Vatican Council reminds us:

> *Since God speaks in Sacred Scripture through men in human fashion, the interpreter of Sacred Scripture, in order to see clearly what God wanted to communicate to us, should carefully investigate what meaning the sacred writers really intended, and what God wanted to manifest by means of their words.* [3]

In his condescension toward humankind, God restricts himself so as to become comprehensible and he dialogues in the language of human beings. Practically, this occurred as men and women of diverse cultures, inspired and enlightened by the Holy Spirit, transmitted to us in the sacred text, the authentic Word of God. The Old Testament took shape over several centuries while the New Testament was written in about sixty years.

The Second Vatican Council is audacious in its reflection and makes an analogical comparison between God's presence in his Word and the very mystery of the incarnation of his Son:

> *. . . For the words of God, expressed in human language, have been made like human discourse, just as the word of the eternal Father, when he took to himself the flesh of human weakness, was in every way made like men.* [4]

In the Bible God speaks to us through human beings and God expresses himself in "human language."

We need to take the two affirmations seriously: **Word of God** and **in human language.** If we fall into a "bipolar" attitude by emphasizing one and de-emphasizing the other, we fail to do justice to Sacred Scripture. Both affirmations are mutually connected. This is the way God reveals himself to humanity.

FUNCTIONS OF THE "HUMAN WORD"

When we reflect on the inspiration of the Canon, we affirm that Scripture is truly God's Word. For now, we will focus on the Bible as the word of men. Let us analyze the functions of the human word.

Language, whether spoken or written, has three main interactive functions. It is necessary to distinguish these three functions for an integral understanding of the Word of God revealed in the human word. The three functions are as follows:

a. **Information**: This function is applicable in relation to nature, the world and history. The word "inform" concerns facts and occurrences, generally through a verb in indicative mood and in third person. It is usually considered objective and adequate for the purposes of science, teaching and historiography. For example, a sign that shows: International Airport 15 mi, is "informing" us that the city has an international airport 15 miles from that particular point.

b. **Expression:** This function deals with the ability of the word to "express" information, and the thought of the person speaking or writing. All who speak or write express themselves; they say something about themselves, they place themselves in the action, they make themselves known. This is considered a subjective action. They express themselves with their tone of voice or their bodily gestures that indicate surprise, joy, fear, anger, or remorse.

c. **Call:** This function is evident in relation to others. The spoken or written word, by its own nature, seeks another; it becomes a link between "you" and "me", a basic principle of all communion. The word not only informs and expresses the inner nature of the person who is speaking or writing, but also seeks a response from the recipient of the communication. This is considered an inter-subjective function wherein one subject appeals to another subject.

The three functions are interconnected and we need to distinguish them in our lives to fully understand the message conveyed to us. Similarly, it is necessary to keep the three functions in mind to fully comprehend the Word of God revealed in human language in the Scripture. To reduce the significance of the human word in the Bible to a mere informative function is impoverishing the communication of the mystery of God hidden in the Sacred Texts. Understanding the human language of Scripture will enable us to respond to the call of the Word. This creative force of calling and responding moves us, enfolds us and liberates us.

FUNCTIONS OF THE HUMAN WORD

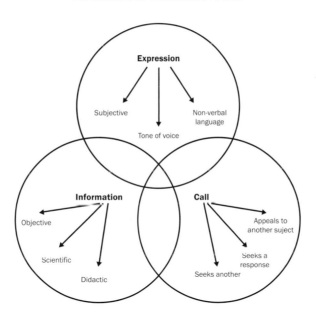

THE THREE FUNCTIONS OF THE WORD IN HOSEA

[1]The Lord says, "When Israel was a child, I loved him and called him out of Egypt as my son. [2]But the more I called to him, the more he turned away from me. My people sacrificed to Baal; they burned incense to idols. [3]Yet I was the one who taught Israel to walk. I took my people up in my

arms, but they did not acknowledge that I took care of them. ⁴I drew them to me with affection and love. I picked them up and held them to my cheek; I bent down to them and fed them. ⁵They refuse to return to me, and so they must return to Egypt, and Assyria will rule them. ⁶War will sweep through their cities and break down the city gates. It will destroy my people because they do what they themselves think best. ⁷They insist on turning away from me. They will cry out because of the yoke that is on them, but no one will lift it from them. ⁸How can I give you up, Israel? How can I abandon you? Could I ever destroy you as I did Admah, or treat you as I did Zeboiim? My heart will not let me do it! My love for you is too strong. ⁹I will not punish you in my anger; I will not destroy Israel again. For I am God and not a mere human being. I, the Holy One, am with you. I will not come to you in anger" (Hosea 11.1-9).

Suggestions with regard to the functions:

a. **Information**: God loves his people in spite of their unfaithfulness. The Lord insists on what he wants, but they turn away. Therefore God could destroy them; but he does not.

b. **Expression**: God reveals himself. He shows abundant mercy: he compares Israel to a child learning to walk; he cares for the child by drawing him with cords of love, embracing him and giving him food to eat. God expresses himself as a mother who deeply loves her child. The Lord expresses himself again when asked whether he would abandon his people. God responds by saying that he can never abandon his people.

c. **Call**: Since we are part of God's people, the Word calls us to respond as we engage with the text. How have we turned away from God? Are we capable of perceiving the maternal traits of the Lord? The Word calls us to respond to God who expresses himself with unending faithfulness.

THE THREE FUNCTIONS OF THE WORD IN THE EPISTLE TO THE ROMANS

[14]**We know that the Law is spiritual; but I am a mortal, sold as a slave to sin.** [15]**I do not understand what I do; for I don't do what I would like to do, but instead I do what I hate.** [16]**Since what I do is what I don't want to do, this shows that I agree that the Law is right.** [17]**So I am not really the one who does this thing; rather it is the sin that lives in me.** [18]**I know that good does not live in me—that is, in my human nature. For even though the desire to do good is in me, I am not able to do it.** [19]**I don't do the good I want to do; instead, I do the evil that I do not want to do.** [20]**If I do what I don't want to do, this means that I am no longer the one who does it; instead, it is the sin that lives in me.** [21]**So I find that this law is at work: when I want to do what is good, what is evil is the only choice I have.** [22]**My inner being delights in the law of God.** [23]**But I see a different law at work in my body—a law that fights against the law which my mind approves of. It makes me a prisoner to the law of sin which is at work in my body.** [24]**What an unhappy man I am! Who will rescue me from this body that is taking me to death?** [25]**Thanks be to God, who does this through our Lord Jesus Christ! This, then, is my condition: on my own I can serve God's law only with my mind, while my human nature serves the law of sin** (Romans 7.14-25).

Suggestions concerning the function of:

   a.   **Information**: This passage shows us Saint Paul's interior struggle with sin and the law. The sinful nature in the apostle does not allow him to do the good that he desires, but he ends up doing the evil that he does not desire. Only God, through Jesus Christ, can free him from this situation, and for that Saint Paul expresses thankfulness.

   b.   **Expression**: Saint Paul reveals his inner nature. If the text were only information, some of the phrases would be rather complex. But if we perceive that the Saint is expressing himself with a tortured heart, our outlook changes. The apostle makes his inner nature known through his struggle between good and evil. He opens his heart and expresses his inner conflict, and acknowledges with gratitude that only Jesus Christ can set him free.

c.   **Call**: The Word here calls us to introspection. The inner conflicts that Paul experienced, we too experience on a daily basis. The Word calls out to each one of us and teaches us to express without fear our inner conflicts.

"ORIGINAL TEXTS" AND "ORIGINAL LANGUAGES" OF THE BIBLE

None of the original manuscripts of any of the books of the Bible have survived. However, we have copies of these manuscripts. The oldest manuscripts of the Bible were written on papyrus or parchment.

Papyrus is made from the stem of the plant. The outer skin is first stripped off. The sticky inner fiber is cut into long strips and placed side by side on a hard surface and hammered into a sheet. The sheet that results is pressed and then dried under pressure. After drying, the sheet of papyrus is polished for use. Papyrus is economical to produce and stable in dry climates, but is not resistant to climatic changes.

Parchment is a thin material made from calfskin, sheepskin or goatskin. The skins are stretched and dried at room temperature, softened with lye and then polished with stone. Parchment has significantly higher durability than papyrus, but it is much more expensive. Parchment manuscripts can be scrubbed, scoured and reused. To form a scroll, a number of sheets are put together. They are placed so that all the horizontal fibers are parallel with the scroll's length on one side and all the vertical fibers are on the other side. Then it is rolled up, resulting in what we call Scripture scrolls or Torah scrolls (if they are scrolls of the books of the Law). It was not until the beginning of the Christian era that codex – sheets of papyrus or folded parchment, were glued or sewn into quires to form what we would today call a notebook or simply a book.

The Bible was originally written in Hebrew, Aramaic and Greek. The Old Testament was written mainly in **Hebrew** with some small portions in **Aramaic** and some full books in **Greek.** The New Testament was written entirely in **Greek**. From these three languages linguists have translated the text into various modern languages. In themselves, these original languages are not sacred languages. Each of them was the common language of communication at the time and within the culture of the human author.

Following are two examples:

An example of Hebrew: Genesis 1.1

בְּרֵאשִׁית בָּרָא אֱלֹהִים אֵת הַשָּׁמַיִם וְאֵת הָאָרֶץ׃

the earth   and   the heavens   God   created   in the   beginning

In the beginning God created the heavens and the earth.

An example of Greek: John 14.6

λέγει αὐτῷ [ὁ] Ἰησοῦς, Ἐγώ εἰμι ἡ ὁδὸς καὶ ἡ ἀλήθεια καὶ ἡ ζωή· οὐδεὶς ἔρχεται πρὸς τὸν πατέρα εἰ μὴ δι' ἐμοῦ.

"I am the way, the truth, and the life; no one goes to the Father except by me."

Sections of the Old Testament only in Aramaic:

- Ezra 4.8-6,18; 7.12-26
- Daniel 2.4b-7.28
- Genesis 31.47
- Jeremiah 10.11

In all there are 640 words in the four books.

Books of the Old Testament Originally in Greek alone:

- Wisdom of Solomon
- 1 Maccabees
- 2 Maccabees
- Baruch
- Judith
- Tobit

These are "deuterocanonical" books added to the canon at a later date from the rest of the Old Testament.

A seventh book, Ecclesiasticus, was thought to be in this same category, but in the 19th and 20th centuries partial Hebrew manuscripts were found. At present we have manuscripts of the entirety of the book of Ecclesiasticus in Greek and approximately two thirds of Ecclesiasticus in Hebrew.

Bible of the Seventy (Septuagint):

This is the name given to the Greek translation of the Hebrew Scriptures that originated in Alexandria and was translated between 300-200 BC. It contains the standard 39 books of the Old Testament canon as well as the deuterocanonical books. The Septuagint is symbolized using "LXX," the Roman numerals for seventy. It is called "of the seventy" because it is believed that 70 or 72 Jewish scholars (six from each tribe of Israel) were commissioned to carry out the task of translating the Hebrew Scripture into Greek, the language most widely used at the time. This is the oldest translation of the Old Testament and is of great value because it aids in understanding the original Hebrew through comparative study.

INSPIRED AND CANONICAL SCRIPTURES

- How is the Bible different from any other type of ancient writing?
- What makes it so unique?
- Why are some books included in the Bible while others are not?
- Why are some books canonical and others apocryphal?
- What is the difference between a "Catholic" and a "Protestant" Bible?
- Who possesses the earliest manuscripts of the Bible?

The answers to these questions require a lot of time and space. The answers will be even lengthier if we analyze the false theories that appear from time to time in the media, theories that claim to be scientific.

How do we respond to all of this?

The answer is: **Holy Scripture is inspired by the Holy Spirit and it is canonical**.

Holy Scripture is a direct affirmation of the belief of the Church handed down by God, through the inspiration of the Holy Spirit. The tradition of the Church is reflected in these inspired and canonical books that were in use from New Testament times. The Scripture constitutes the rule of faith, which leads us to God and allows us to live out the Gospel.

Biblical inspiration is the work of the Holy Spirit. Authors of the sacred texts were divinely inspired. They put into writing the message that God desired to reveal to his people, thus the Bible is the true Word of God.

The **Canon** of the Bible refers to the definitive list of the books which are considered to be divine revelation. The word "canon" means "meter", "norm", "rule" or "pattern." During the first three centuries of the Christian era, the canon was "the rule of faith" by which the disciples of Christ were to live. From the fourth century, in addition to this, it also referred to the "normative element" of the books considered inspired by the Holy Spirit. These books were thus called canonical books because they were accepted by the Church and proposed to believers as the norm of faith and Christian life.

The Church, by the grace of the Holy Spirit and the help of its *Magisterium*, has over time discerned the inspired and canonical books. For a book to be included in the Canon, it had to meet the following three principal criteria:

1. **Apostolic origin**: It did not necessarily have to be written by an apostle, but it had to be a part of the apostolic church.
2. **Extended use**: It had to be in liturgical and pastoral use within the Christian communities that developed as the faith spread throughout the known world.
3. **Conformity with the rule of faith**: The text had to be clear of controversy and in conformity with the essential elements of the life of faith that had been established from the time of the Apostles in Christian communities.

Most Christian churches and confessions adhere to the same canonical books to form the New Testament. However, the situation is different for the Old Testament. The Catholic Church accepts a longer Old Testament canon made up of 46 books derived from the Greek Septuagint (LXX) translation and the Alexandrian Canon. Protestant and Evangelical Christians accept a shorter Old Testament canon of 39 books whose origin is in the Hebrew Palestinian Canon followed by the Jews. The chart below offers a listing of all these plus the canon followed by the Orthodox Church.

BOOKS OF THE OLD TESTAMENT ACCORDING TO THE GREAT TRADITIONS:

Judaism	Protestant	Catholic	Orthodox
Genesis	Genesis	Genesis	Genesis
Exodus	Exodus	Exodus	Exodus
Leviticus	Leviticus	Leviticus	Leviticus
Numbers	Numbers	Numbers	Numbers
Deuteronomy	Deuteronomy	Deuteronomy	Deuteronomy
Joshua	Joshua	Joshua	Joshua
Judges	Judges	Judges	Judges
Ruth	Ruth	Ruth	Ruth
Samuel	I Samuel	I Samuel	I Samuel
	II Samuel	II Samuel	II Samuel
Kings	I Kings	I Kings	I Kings
	II Kings	II Kings	II Kings
Isaiah	Isaiah	Isaiah	Isaiah
Jeremiah	Jeremiah	Jeremiah	Jeremiah
Ezekiel	Ezekiel	Ezekiel	Ezekiel
Chronicles	I Chronicles	I Chronicles	I Chronicles
	II Chronicles	II Chronicles	II Chronicles
Ezra and Nehemiah	Ezra	Ezra	Ezra
	Nehemiah	Nehemiah	Nehemiah
		Tobit	
		Judith	
Esther (w/o Grk. supp.)	Esther (w/o Grk. supp.)	Esther (w/ Grk. supp.)	
		I Maccabees	
		II Maccabees	
			III Maccabees
			IV Maccabees
Job	Job	Job	Job
Psalms	Psalms	Psalms	Psalms
Proverbs	Proverbs	Proverbs	Proverbs
Ecclesiastes	Ecclesiastes	Ecclesiastes	Ecclesiastes
Song of Solomon	Song of Solomon	Song of Solomon	Song of Solomon
		Wisdom of Solomon	
		Ecclesiasticus	Ecclesiasticus
			Psalms of Solomon
Lamentations	Lamentations	Lamentations	Lamentations
		Baruch	
		Epistle to Jeremiah	
Daniel (w/o Grk. supp.)	Daniel (w/o Grk. supp.)	Daniel (w/ Grk. supp.)	Daniel (w/ Grk. supp.)
Hosea	Hosea	Hosea	Hosea
Joel	Joel	Joel	Joel
Amos	Amos	Amos	Amos
Obadiah	Obadiah	Obadiah	Obadiah
Jonah	Jonah	Jonah	Jonah
Micah	Micah	Micah	Micah
Nahum	Nahum	Nahum	Nahum
Habakkuk	Habakkuk	Habakkuk	Habakkuk
Zephaniah	Zephaniah	Zephaniah	Zephaniah
Haggai	Haggai	Haggai	Haggai
Zechariah	Zechariah	Zechariah	Zechariah
Malachi	Malachi	Malachi	Malachi

The abbreviation "w/o Grk. Supp." and "w/ Grk. Supp." means "without Greek supplement" and "with Greek supplement" respectively. The books of Esther and Daniel are two proto-canonical books (introduced in the canon at the outset). Some parts of these basically Hebrew manuscripts have only been found in Greek and are considered deuterocanonical (introduced in the canon at a later date).

THE NEW TESTAMENT ON THE SUBJECT OF INSPIRATION

[14]But as for you, continue in the truths that you were taught and firmly believe. You know who your teachers were [15]and you remember that ever since you were a child, you have known the Holy Scriptures, which are able to give you the wisdom that leads to salvation through faith in Christ Jesus. [16]All Scripture is inspired by God and is useful for teaching the truth, rebuking error, correcting faults, and giving instruction for right living, [17]so that the person who serves God may be fully qualified and equipped to do every kind of good deed (2 Timothy 3.14-17).

> . . . For holy mother Church, relying on the belief of the Apostles (see John 20.31; 2 Tim. 3.16; 2 Peter 1.19-20, 3.15-16), holds that the books of both the Old and New Testaments in their entirety, with all their parts, are sacred and canonical because written under the inspiration of the Holy Spirit, they have God as their author and have been handed on as such to the Church herself.[5]

> The inspired books teach the truth. Since everything asserted by the inspired authors or sacred writers must be held to be asserted by the Holy Spirit, it follows that the books of Scripture must be acknowledged as teaching solidly, faithfully and without error that truth which God wanted put into sacred writings for the sake of salvation.[6]

SAINT AUGUSTINE'S REFLECTION ON THE "MYSTERY" OF BIBLICAL INSPIRATION:

> To explain all that was told to them, in their fullest sense, is beyond all human ability. Moreover, I do not doubt to affirm, my brothers, that perhaps not even Saint John himself was able; he spoke as he could, because he was a man who spoke on God's behalf - inspired, certainly, but always human. Thanks to the inspiration, he was able to say something: if he had not been inspired, he would have been unable to say anything. But although he was inspired he was unable to reveal the whole mystery; he said what a human being could say.[7]

CHAPTER 2

THE WORD OF GOD: INTERPRETING THE BIBLE IN THE TRADITION OF THE CHURCH

BIBLE AND TRADITION: WORD OF GOD

The term "Word of God" has several meanings and these meanings vary with the situation and context. For example, the Bible is the Word of God, and the Son of God, Jesus Christ, is also the Word of God. **"The Word became a human being and, full of grace and truth, lived among us"** (John 1.14a).

> To clearly understand the difference and the intimate relationship between the Word and Scripture, we turn to the Second Vatican Council: "Sacred tradition and Sacred Scripture form one sacred deposit of the Word of God, committed to the Church."[8]

TRADITION

Encounter with God is not limited to the events that are noted in the Bible. Tradition is the perception of God's message that the Church presents to the faithful. God makes known his will through the liturgy, through the *Magisterium* of the Church, through the saints and through various other channels in the life of the church throughout the ages.

All these sources of Tradition, together with sacred Scripture, constitute the Word of God. *The Synod of the Word* convened in October 2008 discussed this subject at length and the following statement was made: *the Word of God precedes and goes beyond the Bible.*[9] This *preceding* and *exceeding* underlines the importance of the Word of God among Catholic Christians.

The Church has always taught that Scripture and Tradition are inseparable. They are mutually dependent on one another. Being attentive to the Word of God means reading the Bible, not in a free and isolated manner, but within the parameters of the Tradition of the Church's life. It is within Mother Church that we comprehend, interpret and apply sacred texts to our life.

Analogy "Verbi Dei"

The expression "Word of God" is analogous. It refers especially to the Word of God in Person, which is the only begotten Son of God, born of the Father before all time, Word of the Father made flesh (cf. John 1.14). The divine Word, already present in the creation of the universe, and especially in the creation of man, has been revealed throughout the history of salvation, and testimony of this is written in the Old and New Testaments. This Word of God transcends Sacred Scripture, although it is contained therein in a unique way. Under the guidance of the Spirit (cf. John 14.26, 16.12-15) the Church guards and maintains it in its living Tradition[10] and offers it to humanity through preaching, the sacraments and the testimony of life. Pastors, therefore, should teach the People of God to embrace the diverse meanings of the expression "Word of God."[11]

BIBLE AND INTERPRETATION

Interpreting the Bible is not a simple matter. Some of the great divisions among Christians over the centuries have come about due to the different and even contradictory interpretations of certain texts of the Bible.

For a Catholic Christian the fundamental platform for interpreting the Bible is from within the Church. Scripture is interpreted according to the Church's faith. There are several reference materials and excellent documents that offer orientation in this matter. The fundamentals of the faith seem quite clear; however, the interpretation of the Bible as it relates practically in the lives of individuals often causes problems.

In the life of the Church there is a basic presupposition: every believer can read and interpret the Bible text for application in his or her own life. However, there are different levels of ability in the interpretation of Sacred Texts. It is here that the *Magisterium* of the Church exercises its responsibility to authentically interpret the Word of God, written or spoken.[12]

In order for God's salvation to reach all humankind, the *Magisterium*, by the grace of the Holy Spirit, listens to the Word of God and expresses it faithfully. When the Church, with the help of tradition and the *Magisterium* interprets Scripture, all believers follow that interpretation and thus apply the Word of God to their lives. This helps them to be more mature Christians.

The Second Vatican Council points out three criteria for correctly interpreting Scripture:

> . . . since Holy Scripture must be read and interpreted in the sacred spirit in which it was written, no less serious attention must be given to the content and unity of the whole of Scripture if the meaning of the sacred texts is to be correctly worked out. The living tradition of the whole Church must be taken into account along with the harmony which exists between elements of the faith. . . .[13]

We will explain each one of these facets:

1. **The Unity of all Scripture**: No text is to be interpreted in isolation from the rest. The Bible is not simply "a book," it is a collection of more than 70 books, composed by different authors, from diverse cultural backgrounds, over several centuries. The Bible is *multiple* in this sense, yet it is *singular and unique*. Within the Bible there is a coherence and unity from the first to the last verse.[14] In Scripture God does not speak to us through a single isolated text but through all the texts within the canon. Each book of the Bible illuminates the others. This explains the progressive nature of Scripture.

2. **The Living Tradition of the Church**: The Bible should be interpreted within the Tradition of the Church. The first and principal framework of the interpretation of Scripture is the life of the Church. The Bible was written within a living community. Therefore it is important to carefully observe how that community lived and continues to live out the Word that is written and placed there by divine inspiration.

3. **Analogy of the Faith**: We cannot separate the interpretation of the Bible from the experience of faith. What we receive through the reading of the Scripture must align with what the Church has in its deposit of faith. No Bible reading should place an individual in conflict with the faith of the Church, for it is the same Holy Spirit who inspired the Scripture and who leads the Church. The Scripture is a book of faith. That can never be discounted at the moment of interpretation.

    It is clear, therefore, that sacred tradition, Sacred Scripture and the teaching authority of the Church, in accord with God's most wise design, are so linked and joined together that one cannot stand without the others, and that all together and each in its own way under the action of the one Holy Spirit contribute effectively to the salvation of souls.[15]

INTERPRETATION AND THE HOLY SPIRIT

The catechism of the Catholic Church recalls the great teaching of the Second Vatican Council – the inseparable relationship between the interpretation of Scripture and the Holy Spirit:

> *But since Sacred Scripture is inspired, there is another and no less important principle of correct interpretation, without which Scripture would remain a dead letter. Sacred Scripture must be read and interpreted in the light of the same Spirit by whom it was written.*[16]

What does it mean to interpret Scripture with the same Spirit by which it was written?

It is the Holy Spirit who inspired the authors to write the Scripture, and who now continues to work in the heart of the believer to rightly interpret Scripture. The Bible is a book of faith, a religious book, a confessional book. Historical analysis of events or knowledge of the literary genre alone is not enough for biblical interpretation. A firm belief and the guidance of the Holy Spirit are necessary as well. It is important to keep in mind the spiritual dimension of Scripture and believe in it as the Word of God or else it becomes dead letters, a lifeless relic of the past without significance for our life today.

The Bible is inspired by the Holy Spirit; therefore it should be read and interpreted with the guidance of the Holy Spirit. This general principle must be kept in mind both in personal reading as well as in group reading; for the *Magisterium* as well as for a group practicing *Lectio Divina*; for the exegete as well as for the catechist. It is the Third Person of the Holy Trinity who enables us to be in harmony with, and experience a truly spiritual reading of, the Bible. Anyone who desires to walk in the truth must open up to the Spirit. The Lord says, in effect: **"When, however, the Spirit comes, who reveals the truth about God, he will lead you into all the truth"** (John 16.13a).

THE HOLY SPIRIT AND THE WORD OF GOD

The Sacred Scriptures, being a gift given by the Holy Spirit to the Church, the Bride of Christ, has its proper hermeneutical abode in the Church. The same Spirit, who is the author of the Holy Scriptures, is also the guide for the proper interpretation in the formation throughout time of the 'fides Ecclesiae.' The Synod recommends the pastors to remind all who are baptized of the role of the Holy Spirit in the inspiration,[17] interpretation and comprehension of the Sacred Scriptures.[18] Consequently, all of us who are disciples are invited to frequently invoke the Holy Spirit, so that He might lead us to a more deep knowledge of the Word of God and the testimony of our faith (cf. John 15.26-27). Remind the faithful that the Sacred Scriptures conclude by evoking the call that is common to both the Spirit and the Bride: "Come, Lord Jesus" (cf. Revelation 22.17,20).[19]

. . . The Bible, however, is also the eternal and divine Word and for this reason requires another understanding, given by the Holy Spirit who unveils the transcendent dimension of the divine Word, present in human words.[20]

THE LITERARY GENRE IN THE PROCESS OF INTERPRETATION

To interpret Scripture correctly, it is important to keep in mind that the Sacred Texts are in a variety of literary genre. The truth is presented in different ways and is expressed in a literary genre that is specific to a particular cultural context and time period. To properly interpret the message of any particular portion of the Bible, one must understand something about the cultural context, the time frame of the writing, as well as the literary style.

There are a variety of literary genres in the Bible. Listed below are a few examples from the Old Testament:

- **Epic stories** (cf. Judges 9.8-15).
- **Dreams and visions** (cf. 1 Kings 3.4-15).
- **Chronicles** (cf. 2 Samuel 2.9-20).
- **Vocational accounts** (cf. Isaiah 6.1-13).

Examples from the New Testament:

- **Parables** (cf. Matthew 13; Luke 15).
- **Controversies** (cf. Mark 11.27-33).
- **Hymns** (cf. Philippians 2.6-11; Colossians 1.15-20).
- **Catalog of vices and virtues** (Romans 1.29-31; Galatians 5.9-21).

    To search out the intention of the sacred writers, attention should be given, among other things, to "literary forms." For truth is set forth and expressed differently in texts which are variously historical, prophetic, poetic, or of other forms of discourse. The interpreter must investigate what meaning the sacred writer intended to express and actually expressed in particular circumstances by using contemporary literary forms in accordance with the situation of his own time and culture. For the correct understanding of what the sacred author wanted to assert, due attention must be paid to the customary and characteristic styles of feeling, speaking and narrating which prevailed at the time of the sacred writer, and to the patterns men normally employed at that period in their everyday dealings with one another.[21]

"…Through the Son, then, God decided to bring the whole universe back to Himself. God made peace through his Son's blood on the cross and so brought back to himself all things, both on earth and in heaven."

(Colossians 1.15-20).

CHAPTER 3

JESUS, THE LIVING WORD

JESUS CHRIST, THE CENTER OF ALL SCRIPTURE

Sacred Scripture is the written Word of God. Jesus Christ is the living Word of God: **"In the past God spoke to our ancestors many times and in many ways through the prophets, but in these last days he has spoken to us through his Son. He is the one through whom God created the universe, the one whom God has chosen to possess all things at the end"** (Hebrews 1.1-2). The God of love "has spoken." Because He is goodness revealed, he makes himself known to humankind. He did it in ancient times through men and women (patriarchs, judges, prophets), and in the fullness of time through his Son, our Lord Jesus Christ, true God and true man.

What relationship exists between the Bible, the written Word of God, and Jesus Christ, the living Word of God?

Saint Jerome says: *To ignore the Scriptures is to ignore Christ.*[22] Blaise Pascal, mathematician, physicist and philosopher of the seventeenth century summarized quite well the relationship between Christ and Scripture in the following phrase: *The entire Bible turns upon Jesus Christ: the Old Testament considers him as its hope, the New as its model, and both as their center.*[23] Take note that Jesus Christ is also the "center" of the Old Testament. Pope Benedict XVI, on April 23, 2009 said to the members of the Pontifical Biblical Commission: *In fact, in spite of the differences between the books that compose it, Sacred Scripture is, in virtue of its unity, of God's design, of which Christ Jesus is the center and the heart (cf. Luke 24.25-27, Luke 24.44-46).*

In its unity the Bible is like a tree that runs its roots in the Old Testament and flowers in the New. Both Testaments find their unity in Jesus Christ. As the living Word of God, Christ is the master key that enables us to unlock the deepest sense of the Scriptures.

On various occasions Jesus is given the title of prophet, which he truly is. But he is not just one among the many prophets that God sent to his people. The Lord is *the Prophet,* since in him all the prophecies are fulfilled. Jesus, as Prophet, is not only the one who transmits the Word of God, but he is *the living and true Word of God.* Jesus, the Word in person, is the ultimate and definitive Word that gives meaning, unity and cohesion to all the other forms of the Word through which God has revealed himself throughout the ages.

It is interesting to reflect on this verse from the First Letter of Peter: **"They tried to find out when the time would be and how it would come. This was the time to which Christ's Spirit in them was pointing, in predicting the sufferings that Christ would have to endure and the glory that would follow"** (1 Peter 1.11). The prophets of the Old Testament are inspired and enlightened by the same Lord Jesus Christ.

The Master is for us the great protagonist of both Testaments. In confronting the Jews, Jesus tells them that the Scriptures (Old Testament) give testimony of him: **"You study the Scriptures, because you think that in them you will find eternal life. And these very Scriptures speak about me! Yet you are not willing to come to me in order to have life"** (John 5.39-40). In another context, in the Gospel of Luke, when he appears following his resurrection, he tells his disciples: **"These are the very things I told you about while I was still with you: everything written about me in the Law of Moses, the writings of the prophets, and the Psalms had to come true"** (Luke 24.44).

In Christ the prophecies of the Old Testament are fulfilled. It is difficult for the disciples to understand, but the Lord himself opens their minds so that they might understand and believe: **"Then he opened their minds to understand the Scriptures"** (Luke 24.45).

To accomplish so great a work, Christ is always present in His Church, especially in her liturgical celebrations. He is present in the sacrifice of the Mass, not only in the person of His minister, "the same now offering, through the ministry of priests, who formerly offered himself on the cross"[24] but especially under the Eucharistic species. By His power He is present in the sacraments, so that when a man baptizes it is really Christ Himself who baptizes.[25] He is present in His word, since it is He Himself who speaks when the holy scriptures are read in the Church. . . [26]

Then, after speaking in many and varied ways through the prophets, "now at last in these days God has spoken to us in His Son" (Hebrews 1.1-2). For He sent His Son, the eternal Word, who enlightens all men, so that He might dwell among men and tell them of the innermost being of God (see John 1.1-18). Jesus Christ, therefore, the Word made flesh, was sent as "a man to men."[27] He "speaks the words of God" (John 3:34), and completes the work of salvation which His Father gave Him to do (see John 5.36; John 17.4). To see Jesus is to see His Father (John 14.9). For this reason Jesus perfected revelation by fulfilling it through his whole work of making Himself present and manifesting Himself: through His words and deeds, His signs and wonders, but especially through His death and glorious resurrection from the dead and final sending of the Spirit of truth. Moreover He confirmed with divine testimony what revelation proclaimed, that God is with us to free us from the darkness of sin and death, and to raise us up to life eternal.[28]

The Word of God is an Unending Spring

Lord, who is able to understand all the richness of a single one of your words? We miss more than we perceive, just as those who are thirsty drink from a spring. The perspectives of the Word of God are so abundant, according to the possibilities of those who study them. The Lord has painted his word with different colors, so that each disciple might contemplate what pleases him. He enclosed in his Word many treasures, so that as each of us meditates, we might discover the riches. He that discovers a part of the treasure does not believe that Word contains only what he found, but understands that he simply found a part of all that is there enclosed. Enriched by the Word, he does not believe that the Word is thus poorer, but understanding that he was unable to perceive all of it, gives thanks because of its great richness. Rejoice because you have overcome, and do not be sad that others have gone further. If you are thirsty, you are happy when you drink, and you are not saddened because you cannot deplete the spring, for if your thirst is satisfied before the spring runs dry, when you are thirsty again you can drink again from it; if, on the contrary, once your thirst is satisfied, the well runs dry, your victory becomes a loss. Give thanks for what you received, and do not be sad for what remains in abundance. What you received, what you enjoyed, is your part; but what remains is your inheritance. What you cannot receive now because of your own weakness, you will be able to receive, if you persevere, at another time. Do not try to drink with greed all at one time that which you cannot consume at one time, nor renounce by negligence what you are able to drink bit by bit.[29]

JESUS CHRIST: THE FACE OF THE WORD OF GOD

Jesus is truly the living Word of God present in the Old and the New Testaments. In the final message of the Synod of Bishops, the Fathers laid out four stages of spiritual journey for a better and fruitful understanding of the light of the Word of God.

- The Voice of the Word: Revelation.
- The Face of the Word: Jesus Christ.
- The Home of the Word: the Church.
- The Ways (or paths) of the Word: the Mission.

For the moment we will concentrate on Jesus Christ as the *Face of the Word of God*.

Jesus Christ, the Second Person of the Holy Trinity, the eternal Word, the true Face of God, enters into time and space and into human history to become one with us. The Word becomes flesh, a human being, so as to interact with human beings in person. In the Final Message (number 4) of the Synod of October 2008, the Fathers state:

> *Therefore the real Jesus Christ is fragile and mortal flesh; he is history and humanity, but he is also glory, divinity, mystery: he who revealed God to us, the God no one has ever seen (cf. John 1.18). The Son of God continues to be so even in the dead body placed in the sepulcher and the resurrection is the living and clear proof to this fact.*[30]

In Jesus Christ, God becomes visible to men. The beautiful Christological hymn of the Letter to the Colossians states that **"Christ is the visible likeness of the invisible God"** (Colossians 1.15a).

- In the Lord, God becomes visible and enters into direct dialogue with humanity.
- The Mystery of the Incarnation places Jesus of Nazareth in a specific time and culture.
- He became incarnate by the work of the Holy Spirit in Mary, the Virgin, and lived a human life like anyone else, but without sin.
- He is the God who is near us.
- He is the true face of the Word of God.
- He is true God and true man making possible an encounter between God and humankind.

Jesus is *the Word* that explains to us *the words* of Scripture. He and he alone can reveal the deeper sense of the Bible. Opening our heart to the Lord is the prerequisite for this deeper revelation. Like the disciples en route to Emmaus, let us allow him to explain the Bible to us. How good it would be to repeat a thousand times over in our life: **"Wasn't it like a fire burning in us when he talked to us on the road and explained the Scriptures to us?"** (Luke 24.32).

Jesus is truly the Face of the Word and, at the same time, he is the authentic "face" of man. The Servant of God, John Paul II, in a beautiful reflection says: *The Church in America should speak more and more of Jesus Christ, the human face of God and the divine face of man.*[31] The Mystery of the Incarnation brings together what is impossible to unite. In Jesus Christ, the living Word of God, the two faces, while different, are united and humankind is granted a picture of life in its fullness. The omnipotent God who is near us, the immutable God who was crucified, the transcendent God who is at the same time historic, is revealed in Jesus Christ, the living Word of God who calls all to participation in the divine life.

God, the inspirer and author of both Testaments, wisely arranged that the New Testament be hidden in the Old and the Old be made manifest in the New.[32] For, though Christ established the new covenant in His blood (see Luke 22.20; 1 Corinthians 11.25), still the books of the Old Testament with all their parts, caught up into the proclamation of the Gospel,[33] acquire and show forth their full meaning in the New Testament (see Matthew 5.17; Luke 24.27; Romans 16.25-26; 2 Corinthians 14.16) and in turn shed light on it and explain it.[34]

What importance does the New Testament have for Christians?

The New Testament, whose central object is Jesus Christ, conveys to us the ultimate truth of divine Revelation. Within the New Testament the four Gospels of Matthew, Mark, Luke and John are the heart of all the Scriptures because they are the principle witness to the life and teaching of Jesus. As such, they hold a unique place in the Church.[35]

**"This cup is God's new covenant sealed with my blood,
which is poured out for you."**
(Luke 22.20b).

"The Word became a human being and, full of grace and truth, lived among us. We saw his glory the glory which he received as the Father's only Son."

(John 1.14a).

CHAPTER 4

MISSIONARY DISCIPLES OF THE LORD: THE SPIRITUALITY OF FOLLOWING CHRIST

I – AN "ENCOUNTER" WITH THE LORD

In recent decades the Church has renewed its emphasis upon the importance of following the Lord. Men and women of every age and all vocations have a "baptismal call" to follow their Lord. Mark the evangelist highlights this very well: **"Then Jesus went up a hill and called to himself the men he wanted. They came to him, [14]and he chose twelve, whom he named apostles. 'I have chosen you to be with me,' he told them. 'I will also send you out to preach'"** (Mark 3.13-14). Here we find the characteristics of Christian identity: to follow Jesus, to be with him, to proclaim his message, and to go out and evangelize. In the terminology of the *Document of Aparecida* we call them: missionary disciples of the Lord.

This insistence on following Christ was particularly stressed in the *Magisterium* of the Holy Father John Paul II. When the beloved Pope launched his proposal to initiate the Third Millennium, in the Apostolic Letter he said:

> First of all, I have no hesitation in saying that all pastoral initiatives must be set in relation to holiness. . . . stressing holiness remains more than ever an urgent pastoral task. . . . this ideal of perfection must not be misunderstood as if it involved some kind of extraordinary existence, possible only for a few "uncommon heroes" of holiness. The ways of holiness

are many, according to the vocation of each individual. . . . The time has come to re-propose wholeheartedly to everyone this high standard of ordinary Christian living: the whole life of the Christian community and of Christian families must lead in this direction. It is also clear however that the paths to holiness are personal and call for a genuine "training in holiness," adapted to people's needs. [36]

In a world of deteriorating values, it is important that the Holy Father should propose the path of holiness as an essential quality for every disciple of Christ at the outset of the Third Millennium! Holiness and following Christ correspond to each other and are essential to the fulfilling of God's calling.

What does it mean to follow the Lord?

What is the scope of the particular call to holiness that God shows us?

What is implied in being a missionary disciple of the Lord?

Let us meditate on the Word of God to enlighten us, beginning with the experience of those who were first called by the Lord in the Gospel according to Saint John:

[35]The next day John was standing there again with two of his disciples, [36]when he saw Jesus walking by. "There is the Lamb of God!" he said.

[37]The two disciples heard him say this and went with Jesus. [38]Jesus turned, saw them following him, and asked, "What are you looking for?"

They answered, "Where do you live, Rabbi?" This word means "Teacher."

[39]"Come and see," he answered. (It was then about four o'clock in the afternoon.) So they went with him and saw where he lived, and spent the rest of that day with him.

[40]One of them was Andrew, Simon Peter's brother. [41]At once he found his brother Simon and told him, "We have found the Messiah" (John 1.35-41).

John the Baptist is with two of his disciples when they see Jesus. The Baptist does not hesitate to point out the one they should follow: Jesus is the Lamb of God. John's followers immediately turn to the Lord. When Jesus sees the two followers he asks them, *"What are you looking for?"* They respond that they want to know where the Lord lives. Jesus then invites them: *"Come and see."* The Lord invites them to encounter him and they spend the rest of that day with him. This is the key to Christianity, to experience and to encounter the Lord.

Pope Benedict XVI says it with great clarity: *Becoming a Christian does not begin with an ethical decision or a great idea, but with an encounter, an event with a Person, that results in a new horizon to life and, with that, a decisive orientation.*[37] It is the Lord Jesus Christ who gives new meaning to a person's life. It is not at all a matter of ethics or Christian morals, but an invitation from the Lord himself to experience a personal encounter. Only a life oriented by the gospel can lead to such a blessed encounter.

Only out of a vital encounter can we strike out on the pathway to authentically follow Christ. When Andrew and his companion encountered Christ it was such an intense experience that it transformed Andrew and his companion into disciples of the Lord. The experience of discipleship is immediately accompanied by a zeal for mission: Andrew is eager to share his joy with his brother Simon. He finds his brother Simon and tells him that he has found the Messiah. What he has seen and heard in his encounter with the Lord is not something about which he can keep quiet and treasure jealously in his own heart. The encounter brings about strength, enthusiasm and a joy that longs to be shared with others: **"We write to you about the Word of life, which has existed from the very beginning. We have heard it, and we have seen it with our eyes; yes, we have seen it, and our hands have touched it. When this life became visible, we saw it; so we speak of it and tell you about the eternal life which was with the Father and was made known to us"** (1 John 1.1-2).

- The first ones called to follow Christ in the Gospel of Saint John reflect a true and concrete testimony to the spirituality of discipleship.
- These few verses that we have just read encourage us to encounter Christ and share the joy of that encounter with others.
- The *Document of Aparecida* defines following Christ as authentic missionary discipleship.
- Discipleship is the only way to be a Christian. It is the only effective method because it was designed and employed by Jesus, the living Word. This is and always has been the teaching of the Church.

The very nature of Christianity consists, therefore, in recognizing the presence of Jesus Christ and following him. That was the wonderful experience of those first disciples who, upon finding Jesus, were fascinated and amazed with the exceptional nature of the one who spoke to them, with the way he dealt with them, corresponding to the hunger and thirst for life that was in their hearts. The evangelist John has registered for us the impact that the person of Jesus produced in the first two disciples that found him, John and Andrew. It all begins with a question: "What are you seeking?" (John 1.38). That question then receives the invitation to share an experience: "Come and see" (John 1.39). This narration will remain in history as a unique synthesis of the Christian method.[38]

THE WORD OF GOD IN THE CHURCH

The Word of God cannot, in any way, remain hidden under a basket; to the contrary, it must be placed at the highest point of the Church, as the best of its adornments. If the Word should remain masked under the letter of the law, as under a basket, it would cease to illuminate men with its eternal light. Hidden under a basket, the Word could not then be a source of spiritual contemplation for those who desire to be free from the seduction of their senses which, with their deception, incline us to perceive only that which is temporal and material: when it is placed, on the other hand, upon the candlestick of the Church, that is to say interpreted by worship in spirit and in truth, the Word of God illuminates all men. The letter, in effect, if it is not interpreted according to its spiritual sense, has no more value than that acquired by the senses and is limited to the material significance of its words, so that the soul is unable to perceive the sense of that which is written. Let us not then place under a basket, with our rational thoughts, the shining lamp (that is to say, the Word that illuminates our intelligence), so that we will not be guilty of having placed under the letter the incomprehensible force of wisdom; let us rather place it on the candlestick (that is to say, on the interpretation given by the Church), in the highest place of genuine contemplation; thus it will illuminate all men with the brightness of the divine revelation.[39]

II – MARY, MOTHER OF THE INCARNATE WORD, EXEMPLARY MODEL FOR FOLLOWING CHRIST

The most holy Virgin Mary is the perfect example of a missionary disciple of the Lord. The first few chapters of the Gospel according to Saint Luke give us a better understanding of the intimate relationship between the Virgin and the Word of God. Pope Benedict XVI says:

> ...*The Magnificat—a portrait, so to speak, of her soul—is entirely woven from threads of Holy Scripture, threads drawn from the Word of God. Here we see how completely at home Mary is with the Word of God, with ease she moves in and out of it. She speaks and thinks with the Word of God; the Word of God becomes her word, and her word issues from the Word of God. Here we see how her thoughts are attuned to the thoughts of God, how her will is one with the will of God. Since Mary is completely imbued with the Word of God, she is able to become the Mother of the Word Incarnate. . . .*[40]

The expressions of the Holy Father about Mary's relationship to the Word are beautiful, true, and at the same time poetic. The Virgin is the woman of the Word to such an extent that everything in her is related to the Word. Her faithfulness to the Word of God is manifested by her submission to the will of God. This is clearly evident in the *Magnificat* as well as in the painful circumstances in the Virgin's life.

The Gospel according to Saint Luke clearly states the attitude of the Virgin's heart as the great mystery of her life unfolds before her. We are told that following the birth of her Son, in the framework of worship and the joy of the angels and the shepherds, Mary kept all that happened in her heart (cf. Luke 2.19). The child Jesus grew in strength and wisdom; and at the age of twelve, he was taken to the Temple. The Scriptures record the encounter between Jesus and the teachers in the temple (cf. Luke 2.41-52). In this context too, **"His mother treasured all these things in her heart"** (Luke 2.51b). Mary lived her life in total obedience to the Divine Word. She was never desperate. She kept, meditated upon and lived out the Word in her own life. Saint Luke records: **". . . how happy are those who hear the word of God and obey it!"** (Luke 11.28).

Mary is an authentic disciple of the Lord because she hears his Word, is obedient to the Word and puts it into practice in her life.

Blessed Mary's faithfulness and exemplary discipleship are magnified by the following examples from the Scripture: The Virgin was the first missionary for Christ as she bore him in her bosom and went to Elizabeth (cf. Luke 1.39-45). She stands at the foot of the cross, with a wounded heart, where she sees her Son tortured and in agony. Here she does not become disheartened, but is faithful to the Word and believes that everything is in accordance with the will of God. The most holy Virgin returns to the apostles praying together after the death and resurrection of the Lord (cf. Acts 1.12-14). After the death of Christ, she bears the presence of Jesus crucified and resurrected for the joy of all humanity. Following the Ascension of her Son she continued to be a disciple and a missionary in the early Christian community.

> The greatest realization of Christian life is the communal life as "children of the Son." Through her faith (cf. Luke 1.45), obedience to the will of God (cf. Luke 1.38), as well as through her constant meditation on the Word and the deeds of Jesus (cf. Luke 2.19.51), the Virgin Mary is the most perfect disciple of the Lord. The Father sends his Word to the world for the salvation of men. Mary, by her faith, becomes the first member of the community of believers in Christ, as well as collaborator in the spiritual renewal of the disciples. From the Gospel emerges the figure of a woman who is free and strong and who consciously strives to truly follow Christ. She has entirely lived the journey of faith as the Mother of Christ and later as a disciple. She was always committed to the will of the Father. Thus she was able to be at the foot of the cross in deep communion, so as to enter fully into the mystery of the Covenant.[41]

MARY: *MATER DEI ET MATER FIDEI*

The Synod, having proposed above all to renew the faith of the Church in the Word of God, looks to Mary, the Virgin Mother of the incarnate Word, who, with her affirmation of the Word of the Covenant and his mission, perfectly fulfills the divine vocation for humanity. The synodal Fathers suggest making known among the faithful the prayer of the *Angelus*, daily memory of the Incarnate Word and the Rosary.

> *The Church of the New Testament lives where the incarnate Word is embraced, loved and served in full commitment to the Holy Spirit. Mary's faith develops later in the love with which she accompanies the growth and the mission of the incarnate Word. Under the cross of the Son, her faith and love become the hope with which Mary accepts her recognition as the Mother of the beloved disciple and of redeemed humanity. The devout and loving attention to the figure of Mary, as model and archetype of the Church's faith, is of capital importance in order to affect today a concrete change in the paradigm in the relationship of the Church to the Word, both in the posture of praying listener as in the generosity of dedication to the mission and the announcement. The synodal Fathers, united with the Holy Father in prayer that the Synod "might bear the fruit of authentic renewal to each Christian community,"[42] invite pastors and the faithful to direct their attention to Mary and ask of the Holy Spirit the grace of a living faith in the Word of God incarnate.[43]*

CHAPTER 5

GENERAL INTRODUCTION TO *LECTIO DIVINA*

I – BRIEF HISTORY OF *LECTIO DIVINA*

Lectio Divina has its origins in Scripture. The history of *Lectio Divina* can be traced from the third century of the Christian era and its development owes much to the monastic movement. *Lectio Divina* is a re-reading of the Scriptures: a biblical text from the past becomes contextualized and applicable in the life of a Christian through prayerful reading. We see individuals, families, groups and communities re-reading earlier texts to shed new light upon a current reality. In liturgical and cultural contexts, in great national events, in the historical sagas, in prophetic reflections, in the kerygmatic proclamations, ancient texts relating the occurrences of the past are re-read. The technical name for this dynamic process of reading texts to relate to current events is called intra-biblical re-reading.

A classic example of intra-biblical re-reading is found in 2 Samuel 7.1-17, the prophecy of Nathan. Here David is promised a temple and a dynastic succession that will be forever permanent (cf. verses 12-16). This theme is repeated on other occasions: in the final words of David (2 Samuel 23.5); in the last words of Solomon's counsel (1 Kings 2.4). The writer of Chronicles repeats it almost verbatim (1 Chronicles 17.1-15).

This theme is repeated in other texts with some variations, for example:

- **"You are my son; today I have become your father. Ask, and I will give you all the nations; the whole earth will be yours"** (Psalm 2.7a-9).

- **"The Lord said to my lord: 'Sit here at my right side until I put your enemies under your feet'"** (Psalm 110.1).

- **". . . I will restore the kingdom of David, . . . and make it as it was long ago"** (Amos 9.11b).

- **". . . Listen, now, descendants of King David. . . the Lord himself will give you a sign: a young woman who is pregnant. . . "** (Isaiah 7.13-14).

- **". . . The time is coming when I will choose as king a righteous descendant of David. That king will rule wisely. . . "** (Jeremiah 23.5a).

In some instances it is the kingdom of David that returns (historically, or in a messianic sense):

- **". . . Israel will once again turn to the Lord their God and to a descendant of David their king"** (Hosea 3.5a).

- **"I, the Lord, will be their God, and a king like my servant David will be their ruler"** (Ezekiel 34.24).

- **"A king like my servant David will be their king. They will all be united under one ruler and will obey my laws faithfully. . . . A king like my servant David will rule them forever"** (Ezekiel 37.24-25).

The examples found in Saint Mark 11.10 and in the cries of the blind man recorded in Saint Mark 10.47-48 give us a better understanding of the messianic title. However, the clearest example in the New Testament is the message of the angel Gabriel to Mary:

"You will become pregnant and give birth to a son, and you will name him Jesus. He will be great and will be called the Son of the Most High God. The Lord God will make him a king, as his ancestor David was, and he will be the king of the descendants of Jacob forever; his kingdom will never end!" (Luke 1.31-33).

We must keep in mind that allusions to the Old Testaments in the New Testament are not merely isolated proof texts. Rather, when an Old Testament passage is quoted by a New Testament author, it brings with it its entire setting in its original usage. Thus, identifying intertextual fragments not only enriches our understanding of the later text, it also allows us to reread the old text in a new light. The old text has shaped the formation of the new, even as the new reshapes the interpretation of the old. This phenomenon of linking the basic texts with a new reading in later times is sometimes called intertextuality. Intertextuality uses Scripture to interpret Scripture by listening for quotations, echoes, and allusions to other inter-canonical texts. It is a form of inner-biblical exegesis. Intertextuality includes explicit quotations (e.g., quotations of the Old Testament in the New Testament), as well as more subtle uses of texts.

Throughout this journey we have gotten a sense of the real force behind the reading, meditation and prayer in the lives of the "authors" of Scriptures.

It can be said that the Bible, from its beginnings has been:
- **Prayer and updating**
- **Interpretation and explanation**

The Bible is, from its origin, an experience of *Lectio Divina* in a broader but real sense of the term. For that reason, there is no prayer more biblical in its content and structure than *Lectio Divina*.

With this understanding in mind, we will focus on a brief description of the prayerful reading of the Bible. Origen (approx. 185-254) was the first to use the term *Lectio Divina*. He stressed the importance of attention, perseverance and prayer for a contemplative reading of the Bible. The Greek expression that Origen used was *Theía Anagnosis*.

From the third century, *Lectio Divina* became the center of monastic and religious life. The monastic establishments of Saint Pachomius (290-351), Saint Basil (330-379), Saint Augustine (354-430) and Saint Benedict (480-547) practiced *Lectio Divina* together with the liturgy and manual labor. These three practices became an integral part of monastic life.

The systematization of *Lectio Divina* into four steps dates from the twelfth century. Around the year 1150, Guigo II, a Cartesian monk, wrote a book entitled *Scala Claustralium*, popularly translated as "Ladder of Monks." In it the "four steps" that lead to union with God: **reading**, **meditation**, **prayer** and **contemplation** are clearly articulated. These steps helped a monk make his way from earth to heaven.

From the twelfth century on, *Lectio Divina* has continued to live and influence various aspects of ecclesial life. With the awakening of the biblical and liturgical movements shaped by the Second Vatican Council, the influence of *Lectio Divina* has increased even more.

> *. . . In effect,* **Reading** *is the careful inspection of the Scriptures with a docile spirit.* **Meditation** *is the concentrated application of the mind that investigates with the help of its own reason the understanding of the hidden truth.* **Prayer** *is the fervent inclination of the heart to God so as to avoid evil and obtain that which is good.* **Contemplation** *is the elevation of the mind fixed on God that tastes the joys of eternal sweetness.*
>
> *Having thus described the four steps we now consider their function. Reading seeks the pleasure of a happy life, meditation finds it, prayer requests it, contemplation experiences it. For God himself said: Seek and you shall find, call and it shall be opened to you (Matthew 7.7). Seek by reading and you will find by meditating, call by prayer and it shall be opened to you by contemplation. Reading places bites in your mouth, prayer draws out the flavor, contemplation is the very sweetness that rejoices and refreshes. Reading remains in the bark, meditation penetrates the substance, prayer by petition fills the desire, and contemplation is the enjoyment of the acquired sweetness. . .* [44]

The Second Vatican Council does not specifically develop the subject of *Lectio Divina*. However, in the Constitution *Dei Verbum*, especially number 25, there is a return to the basic principles of the prayerful reading of the Bible. From then on the spiritual biblical development increased significantly in different parts of the world.

> *Which of you, I ask, if requested to recite a psalm is able to do so, or any other part of Sacred Scripture? In truth, none of you! And that is not the worst of it; for in fact you are lazy concerning spiritual matters. . . And what is your defense against such an accusation? You respond: I am not a monk; rather I have a wife and children and I need to take care*

of my domestic responsibilities. Yet precisely for that reason everything is going awry: for you have persuaded yourselves that only monks should be concerned with Lectio Divina, *when it fact you need it more than they do. Those that walk in the open fields and receive wounds each day are those who most need medicine. So that it is a much greater evil to consider useless* Lectio Divina, *than simply to not read the Scriptures.*[45]

Therefore, all the clergy must hold fast to the Sacred Scriptures through diligent sacred reading and careful study, especially the priests of Christ and others, such as deacons and catechists who are legitimately active in the ministry of the word. This is to be done so that none of them will become "an empty preacher of the word of God outwardly, who is not a listener to it inwardly" since they must share the abundant wealth of the divine word with the faithful committed to them, especially in the sacred liturgy. The sacred synod also earnestly and especially urges all the Christian faithful, especially Religious, to learn by frequent reading of the divine Scriptures the "excellent knowledge of Jesus Christ" (Phil. 3.8). "For ignorance of the Scriptures is ignorance of Christ." Therefore, they should gladly put themselves in touch with the sacred text itself, whether it be through the liturgy, rich in the divine word, or through devotional reading, or through instructions suitable for the purpose and other aids which, in our time, with approval and active support of the shepherds of the Church, are commendably spread everywhere. And let them remember that prayer should accompany the reading of Sacred Scripture, so that God and man may talk together; for "we speak to Him when we pray; we hear Him when we read the divine saying."[46]

II – *LECTIO DIVINA* IN SOME TEXTS OF JOHN PAUL II, BENEDICT XVI AND IN THE DOCUMENT OF APARECIDA

The *Magisterium* of the Church, taking into consideration the needs of the time, realized the importance of recovering *Lectio Divina* as the Second Vatican Council drew to a close. In this chapter we want to concentrate on some of the discourses of John Paul II, Benedict XVI, as well as the conclusive *Document of Aparecida* that make direct reference to the practice of *Lectio Divina*.

> *"I am the Way, the Truth and the Life" (Jn 14.6). With these words, Jesus presents himself as the one path which leads to holiness. But a specific knowledge of this way comes chiefly through the word of God which the Church proclaims in her preaching. Therefore, the Church in America "must give a clear priority to prayerful reflection on Sacred Scripture by all the faithful."[47] This reading of the Bible, accompanied by prayer, is known in the tradition of the Church as* Lectio Divina, *and it is a practice to be encouraged among all Christians. For priests, the* Lectio Divina *must be a basic feature of the preparation of their homilies, especially the Sunday homily.[48] . . . [49]*

In light of the above Scripture passage from the Gospel according to Saint John, the Pope introduces the subject of holiness. The Holy Father says that it is necessary for all the faithful to enter into the dynamics of "prayerful reflection" of the Sacred Scripture. How is that done? The Servant of God says: "through *Lectio Divina*, the prayerful reading of the Bible."

John Paul II insisted that the practice of *Lectio Divina* is an essential element in the spiritual life of the priest, especially in the preparation of Sunday homilies.

> *There is no doubt that this primacy of holiness and prayer is inconceivable without a renewed listening to the word of God. Ever since the Second Vatican Council underlined the pre-eminent role of the word of God in the life of the Church, great progress has certainly been made in devout listening to Sacred Scripture and attentive study of it. Scripture has its rightful place of honour in the public prayer of the Church. Individuals and communities now make extensive use of the Bible, and among lay people there are many who devote themselves to Scripture with the valuable*

help of theological and biblical studies. But it is above all the work of evangelization and catechesis which is drawing new life from attentiveness to the word of God. Dear brothers and sisters, this development needs to be consolidated and deepened, also by making sure that every family has a Bible. It is especially necessary that listening to the word of God should become a life-giving encounter, in the ancient and ever valid tradition of Lectio Divina, which draws from the biblical text the living word which questions, directs and shapes our lives.[50]

At the beginning of the Third Millennium Pope John Paul II insisted that all Christians must strive to live a life of holiness. Holiness can take primary place in a believer's life only by a renewed listening to the Word of God. The Pope appreciated the growth of the people in holiness since the time of the Council. The Scriptures are now present in the life of the Church and many, especially lay people, are dedicated to its study and reflection. John Paul II insisted on the need to *consolidate and deepen* scriptural orientation. He clearly proposed *Lectio Divina* as a means of encounter with the Word, an encounter that should model, orient and move the life of the believer.

In this context, I would like in particular to recall and recommend the ancient tradition of Lectio Divina: *the diligent reading of Sacred Scripture accompanied by prayer brings about that intimate dialogue in which the person reading hears God who is speaking, and in praying, responds to him with trusting openness of heart.*[51] *If it is effectively promoted, this practice will bring to the Church - I am convinced of it - a new spiritual springtime. As a strong point of biblical ministry,* Lectio Divina *should therefore be increasingly encouraged, also through the use of new methods, carefully thought through and in step with the times. It should never be forgotten that the Word of God is a lamp for our feet and a light for our path (cf. Psalm 119[118].105).*[52]

A few months after the initiation of his Petrine Ministry, Benedict XVI recommended *Lectio Divina* as a means of dialogue between God and man, and between man and God. He said that an intensive practice of *Lectio Divina* would usher in "a new spiritual springtime in the Church." This is truly encouraging and underlines the need for the prayerful reading of the Bible. He also points out how *Lectio Divina* could be adapted to the present day and age with new methods for biblical pastoral orientation. Thus he upholds tradition, yet effectively adjusted to pastoral needs.

> . . . *thinking with the thought of Christ. And we can do this by reading the holy Scripture where the thoughts of Christ are Words that speak with us. In this sense we should follow the "Lectio Divina", listening in the Scriptures to the thought of Christ, learning to think with Christ, thinking with the thought of Christ and thus having the same feelings of Christ, being capable of giving Christ's thought and feelings to others. . .* [53]

Speaking to the bishops of the Synod on the Eucharist, the Pope presented *Lectio Divina* in a Christological context. He pointed out the centrality of Christ in Scripture. He reminded the bishops that the prayerful reading of Scripture centered in Christ allows for the sharing of the thoughts and sentiments of Christ himself to others.

> *Among the many fruits of this biblical springtime I would like to mention the spread of the ancient practice of* Lectio Divina *or "spiritual reading" of Sacred Scripture. It consists in pouring over a biblical text for some time, reading it and rereading it, as it were, "ruminating" on it as the Fathers say and squeezing from it, so to speak, all its "juice," so that it may nourish meditation and contemplation and, like water, succeed in irrigating life itself. One condition for* Lectio Divina *is that the mind and heart is illumined by the Holy Spirit, that is, by the same Spirit who inspired the Scriptures, and that they be approached with an attitude of "reverential hearing."* [54]

The Holy Father Benedict XVI spoke of a biblical "springtime" with regard to the practice of *Lectio Divina*. He reflected on the traditional prayer of the Angels and describes the prayerful reading of the Bible graphically. He used evocative expressions for the spiritual reading of Scripture like: "ruminating . . . squeezing from it the juice . . . irrigating life itself." He insisted on the need to be enlightened by the Holy Spirit through "reverential hearing."

My dear young friends, I urge you to become familiar with the Bible, and to have it at hand so that it can be your compass pointing out the road to follow. By reading it, you will learn to know Christ. Note what Saint Jerome said in this regard: "Ignorance of the Scriptures is ignorance of Christ"(PL 24,17; cf Dei Verbum, 25). A time-honoured way to study and savour the word of God is Lectio Divina *which constitutes a real and veritable spiritual journey marked out in stages. After the* **lectio**, *which consists of reading and rereading a passage from Sacred Scripture and taking in the main elements, we proceed to* **meditatio**. *This is a moment of interior reflection in which the soul turns to God and tries to understand what his word is saying to us today. Then comes* **oratio** *in which we linger to talk with God directly. Finally we come to* **contemplatio**. *This helps us to keep our hearts attentive to the presence of Christ whose word is "a lamp shining in a dark place, until the day dawns and the morning star rises in your hearts"(2 Peter 1.19). Reading, study and meditation of the Word should then flow into a life of consistent fidelity to Christ and his teachings.*[55]

It is surely worth reading and reflecting upon all of Pope Benedict XVI's final message to the World Youth Meeting in 2006, but here we will only comment briefly on the paragraph regarding *Lectio Divina*.

The Pope urged the youth to be familiar with the Bible and proposed having it at hand as a compass to guide them through the path of life. He also insisted on the Christological centrality of Scripture by quoting Saint Jerome, mentioned in the Second Vatican Council's *Dei Verbum* 25a.

Then he proposed *Lectio Divina* as the principal pathway to journey into and taste the riches of the Word of God. He defined it as a "valid and appropriate spiritual journey in stages." He described each of the four steps of *Lectio Divina* and exhorts the youth to act.

Among the many ways of approaching the Sacred Scripture, there is a privileged one to which we are all invited: Lectio Divina *or exercise of prayerful reading of the Sacred Scripture. This prayerful reading, well practiced, leads to an encounter with Jesus the Teacher, to the knowledge of the mystery of Jesus the Messiah, to fellowship with Jesus the Son of God, and to the testimony of Jesus, Lord of the universe. With its four steps (reading, meditation, prayer, contemplation), prayerful reading encourages a personal encounter with Jesus Christ in the same way as with so many other persons found in the Gospel: Nicodemus and his desire for eternal life (cf. John 3.1-21), the Samaritan woman and her longing for true worship (cf. John 4.1-42), the man born blind and his desire for inner light (cf. John 9), Zacchaeus and his longing to change (cf. Luke 19.1- 10). All of them, because of this encounter, were illuminated and refreshed because they opened up to the experience of the Father's mercy that is offered through his Word of truth and life. They didn't open their heart to something about the Messiah, but to the very Messiah, the pathway of growth in maturity conformed to the fullness (cf. Ephesians 4.13), the process of discipleship, fellowship with brothers and sisters and social commitment.*[56]

As the final text of the *Magisterium* of the Church in this section, we will look at the *Document of Aparecida* in relation to *Lectio Divina*. Among the many ways of approaching the Scriptures, *Lectio Divina* is considered the privileged one and the one to which all are invited. John Paul II and Benedict XVI stated that *Lectio Divina* emphasizes the centrality of Christ. Through *Lectio Divina* there is an encounter with, the knowledge of, fellowship with and the testimony of Christ.

Document of Aparecida 249 provides us with examples of personal encounters with Jesus Christ taken from the Scripture: Nicodemus, the Samaritan woman, the man born blind and Zacchaeus. All those who encountered Christ were illuminated and refreshed because they opened their hearts to the Messiah. Such encounter is the path to growth in authentic discipleship, fellowship with the brethren, and commitment to society.

III – SOME OTHER DEFINITIONS AND DESCRIPTIONS OF *LECTIO DIVINA*

The reflection on the Magisterial texts which we have already done has given us ample definitions and descriptions of *Lectio Divina*. To those we add three more definitions that will enrich our understanding through the facets they point out and by the authority of those who share them.

We begin with the definition by Cardinal Carlos Maria Martini, Archbishop Emeritus of Milan: *Lectio Divina is the systematic exercise of giving personal attention to the Word.*[57] It is a brief definition, but one in which every word is significant. Let us reflect on each word.

- **Exercise**: activity, movement, commitment, effort
- **Systematic**: ordered steps, method, dynamic
- **Attention**: not only hearing, also response, need for silence
- **Personal**: our own history and circumstances, our heart
- **Word**: Bible in the Church, Jesus Christ

The second definition is taken from the former Abbot General of the Cistercian Order, Bernardo Olivera (OCSO): *Lectio Divina is a personal reading of the Word of God through which one makes an effort to assimilate its truth and life; done in faith, in a spirit of prayer, believing in the real presence of God who speaks to us through the sacred text.*[58] This definition is more descriptive and stresses the importance of the theological dimension of *Lectio Divina*: faith, the real presence of God, and the sacred text speaking to us.

The final definition is taken from the document of the Pontifical Biblical Commission. *The Interpretation of the Bible in the Church* offers the following: *Lectio Divina is a reading, on an individual or communal level, of a more or less lengthy passage of Scripture, received as the word of God and leading, at the prompting of the Spirit, to meditation, prayer and contemplation.*[59]

This is a more descriptive definition in that it includes both possible forms of *Lectio Divina*, personal and communal, and the four classic steps as well.

Knowledge of the different definitions and descriptions of *Lectio Divina* enriches us. It is useful to continue reading and investigating other works and other authors for an even broader and deeper understanding.

Many definitions speak of the method of *Lectio Divina*. We suggest that throughout the centuries in the life of the Church, *Lectio Divina* has been more than a method. It would be accurate to speak of *Lectio Divina* as a tradition or as a current of spiritual life in the Church that incorporates various methods. This will free us from any single, narrow understanding and provide the liberty to incorporate all the essential elements of *Lectio Divina*.

While embracing these elements we should also be free and open to other methods that help us achieve the objective of *Lectio Divina* – which is to enter into dialogue with the Lord through Scripture. These other methods may change with time and will be replaced by newer methods depending on the needs of the Church. We must always keep in mind the special needs of those who are directly involved in the practice of *Lectio Divina*. Depending upon cultural distinctiveness, the age of the individuals and the level of church background, certain methods and resources will be more appropriate than others in reaching the objective of *Lectio Divina*, that is, for the individual to enter into fellowship with God who speaks to us in his Word.

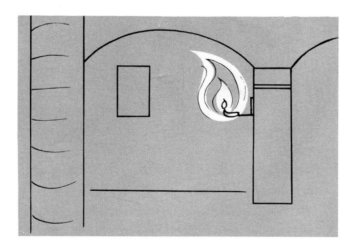

"Your Word is a lamp to guide me, and a light for my path."
(Psalm 119.105).

"You will become pregnant and give birth to a son, and you will name
him Jesus. He will be great and will be called the Son of the Most High
God. The Lord God will make him a king, as his ancestor David was,
and he will be the king of the descendants of Jacob forever;
his kingdom will never end!"

(Luke 1.31-33).

CHAPTER 6

THE STEPS OF *LECTIO DIVINA*

Over the years *Lectio Divina* has had as few as three and as many as eight steps, depending upon the prevailing school of thought. Here we will concentrate on five steps, as these are generally accepted within the framework of biblical and pastoral orientation. The other methods do not differ greatly from the basic practice we will offer. The differences have more to do with grouping steps together or dividing steps for the purpose of further describing specific elements in the practice of *Lectio Divina*.

I – FIRST STEP: READING

Prior to reading Scripture, there are three essential elements that should always be considered: choice of the time and place, choice of the biblical text to be read, and the invocation of the Holy Spirit. The first element is practical, the second is spiritual and the third theological. Ignoring these prerequisites will hinder the successful outcome of the practice of *Lectio Divina*. Let us look at each one briefly.

1. **Time and Place.**
    The choice of the time is absolutely personal and determined by each individual. For a fruitful realization of *Lectio Divina*, twenty minutes is the minimum. The optimum would be about fifty minutes. Beyond an hour could lead to fatigue and a lapse of concentration. In the case of communal *Lectio Divina*, the number of participants plays a key role in determining the time. It should be between sixty and ninety minutes. Over two hours could lead to exhaustion and lapse of focus. Choosing a space is personal and depends on

the possibilities of each individual or group. A place that is quiet and calm is the most ideal. Cellular phones, televisions, computers and other electronic devices need to be switched off so that the mind and heart can concentrate solely on God who reveals himself in his Word. A church in which there is no liturgical function at the time of *Lectio Divina* is one of the most appropriate places. Seated on a bench near the altar or near a significant religious image would provide a conducive atmosphere for *Lectio Divina*. At home, chose a quiet place where you will not be interrupted. If this is not possible, you could perhaps use a chapel or a room in the parish you attend. Another alternative is to choose a comfortable place in the open air, a quiet park or plaza. To practice *Lectio Divina* while contemplating a meadow, a mountain or the sea can be quite refreshing. To create an ideal atmosphere for *Lectio Divina*, one may need to be innovative to discover the best location, as well as responsive to religious sensitivity.

2. **Bible Text.**
   The choice of the Bible passage beforehand is fundamental to *Lectio Divina* so that no time is wasted when the moment of prayer is at hand. If the text has not been chosen we run the risk of endlessly scanning through the pages of the Bible. When selecting the text there are several options. Passages may be selected based upon a subject. For example, we can pray and reflect on our vocation and then look up texts that refer to that subject. Or we can engage in a systematic reading of a specific book of the Bible. These options are valid and interesting. However, the easiest and perhaps most helpful way to select the text may be to follow the liturgical calendar of the Church. Here, the one who is praying does not choose the text. Rather it is God who does so through the liturgical life of the Church. Normally, prayer is concentrated on the Gospel reading, however in some cases the first reading and/or the Psalm may be included in the exercise of *Lectio Divina*.

3. **Holy Spirit.**

The invocation of the Holy Spirit is the actual entrance into *Lectio Divina*. It is fundamental to enter into the reading of the Scripture with faith. We are not studying history, nor are we reading the Sacred Text out of curiosity. We read the text because it is the Word of God and it impacts our lives. The same Holy Spirit who inspired the sacred authors is today in our hearts and we read the Bible believing it is God's Word. It is therefore necessary to be silent and seek the mysterious presence of God's Holy Spirit who shows us how to pray as we should. Silence, inner focus, spiritual contemplation, the memory of our baptism as the door for the Spirit into our hearts – we should keep these things in mind as we begin the prayerful reading of a Scripture text. We can use prayers, hymns or songs that invoke the Holy Spirit.

INVOCATION OF THE HOLY SPIRIT

Come, Holy Spirit,
fill the hearts of your faithful ones
and light the fire of your love in us.

V. Send your Spirit, and all will be created.
R. And populate the face of the earth.

Let us pray:

Oh God, who has enlightened
the hearts of your children
with the light of the Holy Spirit;
make us receptive to your inspiration,
so as to always be nourished with that which is good
and to rejoice in your refreshing
through Jesus Christ our Lord,
Amen.

The Holy Spirit prays in us:

"In the same way the Spirit also comes to help us, weak as we are. For we do not know how we ought to pray; the Spirit himself pleads with God for us in groans that words cannot express. And God, who sees into our hearts, knows what the thought of the Spirit is; because the Spirit pleads with God on behalf of his people and in accordance with his will" (Romans 8.26-27).

"Those who are led by God's Spirit are God's children. For the Spirit that God has given you does not make you slaves and cause you to be afraid; instead, the Spirit makes you God's children, and by the Spirit's power we cry out to God, "Father! my Father!" God's Spirit joins himself to our spirits to declare that we are God's children" (Romans 8.14-16).

Once we have decided on a time and place, selected a Scripture passage and invoked the Holy Spirit, we initiate the step of reading. The question that should guide us in this first step of *Lectio Divina* is:

What does the text say?

What is its objective? What does it affirm? What does it reject? What does it question? What is its strength? What does it confront?

It is important to read the Bible text two or three times. Reading aloud once and a second time silently is helpful. It is also important to try to identify the literary genre. This in no way demands a sophisticated literary study, but only an effort to determine the general writing style. Sometimes this is clear as in the case of a parable or a miracle. On other occasions it may be difficult to discover the proper genre. Whenever possible, it is important to compare the text with other translations in the same language. This will allow for appreciation of different expressions of a particular passage that will illuminate our understanding.

Why is the literary genre important?

Genre is important because it helps us discover the message the Word wants to communicate. For example, the parables convey various aspects of the kingdom of heaven. The healing ministry of the Lord makes reference not only to the physical healing, but also to the salvation that the Lord brings through the curing of the soul that is sick with sin. These aspects are important for a better understanding of the biblical text.

Once we have determined the literary genre we can approach the text in different ways. Here are a few ways that may be helpful.

1. **Determine the characters involved**: A character is any individual or group of individuals involved in some action in the text. There are individual characters: Jesus, Pilate, etc. Others are collective characters: the people; the scribes; etc. In some cases, they appear with pronouns that do not make direct reference to someone present in the text: "they;" "those who were present." Some questions that can give us orientation are: How many people appear in the text? How are they mentioned? How many times does the same person appear throughout the account?

2. **Detect the actions of the characters**: What does each person do in the narrative? Here we must give particular attention to the verbs: he looked; she entered; they left; they were amazed. Particularly note the verbs that describe the specific actions of the characters mentioned in the account.

3. **Take note of the places and the spaces**: Where does the action take place? References to places and spaces: on the way; in the boat; on the mountain; on the plain.

4. **Visualize the references to time**: At what time of day does the action take place? At times, a few verses describe a week's activity. In other cases, a lengthy account describes action taking place within a few minutes. Typical references in the Gospels: in the morning; in the evening; the first day of the week; when everything was dark, it was night; when they were alone.

5. **Narrators and dialogues**: Who narrates the text? Jesus? The evangelist? Another character? This changes from narrative to narrative. Are there dialogues between persons? At what time? Why? Is the direct style predominant? All these questions help us to delve into what the Word of God wants to say to us today.

6. **Subdivide the text**: With the various elements that are gathered, one can make a tentative subdivision of the account in two or more parts. These would be like scenes in a play. The criteria to determine the divisions spring out from each event.

7. **Understand the central point and the resolution**: In general, every account has an introduction, a central point and a conclusion. For *Lectio Divina* it is important to detect the central point: Where is the issue situated? What is the heart of the subject that needs resolving? This is the central point, the heart of the text. From that point on we need to concentrate on the resolution. Some accounts have more than one central point.

8. **Essential and secondary elements**: In a narrative there are essential elements without which the plot disintegrates, making it impossible to determine both the central issue and the resolution. There are secondary aspects. These give color to the text, and even if they are eliminated it would not affect the plot, the central point or the resolution.

9. **Texts within the text**: It is quite common for texts of the New Testament to contain quotes from the Old Testament. We ask ourselves then: What is the text that is quoted? (Check footnotes for Old Testament references). What place does this new text occupy within the complete account? Why does the author use this quote here?

All the elements just described help us to experience a more fruitful and comprehensive reading of the text – the first step of *Lectio Divina*. Not all of these will be applied to any given text. That will depend on the nature of the passage. A lengthy discourse of Jesus in the Gospel of Saint John is not the same as the description of one of our Lord's miracles in the Gospel of Saint Mark.

During the first reading of the text, when you begin to analyze the passage, it is often helpful to read again with a pencil and paper in hand. It can be beneficial to have the Bible text printed or photocopied so that notes can be made and interesting passages can be highlighted.

BIBLICAL MEMORY

When you analyze a Scripture passage, other passages from the Bible may come to mind which are similar or relate to the subject. This is known as *biblical memory*. If this occurs while you are reading, it is useful to turn to the passage or passages in order to corroborate your first intuition. Interesting inter-textual relationships can thus be established that are helpful in the comprehension, interpretation and application of the Word of God to your life.

For example:

When reading the parable of the merciful father (Luke 15.11-32), upon reaching verse 20 one finds the following suggestive section that occurs at the Father's first glimpse of his returning son: "his father saw him; his heart was filled with pity, and he ran, threw his arms around his son, and kissed him." A careful and diligent reader of Sacred Scripture will possibly recognize that the same evangelist, Saint Luke, uses similar phraseology in another narrative, the parable of the Good Samaritan (Luke 10.30-37), where we read in verse 33: "when he saw him, his heart was filled with pity." The same verb translated "to see" and "to have pity," is used in both passages. One text can illuminate the other; the attitudes and actions of one character feed those of the other. This is what we mean by using biblical memory to strengthen the understanding of Scripture.

SUGGESTIONS FOR COMMUNAL READING OF SCRIPTURE

When *Lectio Divina* is practiced in a group setting, different ways of reading the Bible text may be used. The coordinator or leader should look at the text beforehand to determine a creative means of reading.

For example:

The first reading may be done aloud by a single person.

The second reading may be done by each one in silence, using his or her own text.

The third reading can be done between two, three or more participants. Depending on the kind of text it is, the leader can assign roles to different readers.

When using *Lectio Divina* with children, it is especially helpful to include a dramatic presentation of the biblical material. Images can greatly strengthen how we perceive and remember what is read or heard.

VALUES PRESENTED IN THE GOSPEL TEXTS

The final analysis of the reading will enable you to point out the positive and negative values found in the biblical text. This is clearly the principal object of the first step of *Lectio Divina*.

Examples of Positive Values

- **God's attitude toward human beings**: mercy and compassion; respect for freedom; comfort and protection; forgiveness without reserve; unconditional love.

- **Our attitude toward God**: the response of faith; praise; confidence in his gracious presence; worship and celebration to honor his holy Name; listening and obedience; devotion; desire that his will be fulfilled in our lives.

- **Attitude of human beings toward each other**: justice; respect; care and protection of the poor and abandoned; forgiveness; dialogue; friendship; care for the family; national pride; openness to strangers.

Examples of Negative Values

- **Of human beings toward God**: not following his ways; not applying obedience to faith; lack of hope and confidence; rejection of his presence; impious attitudes; failure to worship him; turning away from his presence; not allowing yourself to be loved or forgiven.

- **Of human beings toward each other**: vengeance; hatred; spite; treason; sexual immorality; uncontrolled fanaticism; lack of sensitivity toward the poor; disgracing others; discord and wrath; enmity.

Examples of positive and negative values give us the key to the second step in the prayerful reading of the Bible. If *Lectio Divina* is personal, what has been analyzed will remain in the heart of each individual. If it is communal, all will share with each other what he or she has discovered in the text and be mutually enriched. What another has discovered enriches me and what I have discovered enriches others. In the case of several participants, it is easier to focus on the central points of the passage as everyone shares what they have discovered in the reading.

The first step of *Lectio Divina* – reading – interprets the Sacred Text as its principal objective. Thus it is good to consider and review what was mentioned in earlier chapters regarding the interpretation of the Bible in the living Tradition of the Church, as regulated by the *Magisterium*.

II – SECOND STEP: MEDITATION

Meditation has had a rich presence in the Church's faith and practice throughout the centuries. It is the second step of prayerful reading of the Bible in the context of Christian thought.

The questions that must guide our meditation are:

What does the text say to me?

We could put this another way by asking: What does God *say to me* in the text? What does he *reveal to me* in this text? What is it that *impacts me* in a special way today?

At this point one begins to consider the positive and negative values discovered in the text. One confronts them in his or her own life and considers how they are lived out.

What is in my heart, and what is missing from my analysis of the text?

We need to respond according to our present situation. Perhaps as recently as a few months or even weeks earlier we would have answered in one way, but given present circumstances we would respond differently today.

Let us remember that here too it is the Holy Spirit who continues to accompany us. The presence of God is at work within us to bring the light of the Scriptures to illuminate our immediate situation and need.

In light of the Word, we will be able to determine the positive aspects of our Christian life. We will also be confronted by our faults and sins. In some ways, the step of meditation is like an examination of our conscience in the light of the text of Scripture. What we read in the former step resounds now in our lives and in our hearts.

When should we progress from reading to meditation, and then to prayer?

There are no fixed rules. The individual who is praying through the Word will perceive, understand and decide at what moment to move on to the next step. Just as the change of seasons are a gradual transition, in the same way we move from one step to another in *Lectio Divina*. When we perceive that our heart is prepared, then we should take the next step.

When *Lectio Divina* is practiced in community, each participant should share, as much as possible, what God has said to him or her in a particular way through the text. It is important to respect the sensitivity and inner awareness of each member of the group. We should not make public intimate personal or family matters. This step should not be a venue for venting personal problems or difficulties with others. (Once the group has been together for a while and has grown to trust one another, it may be appropriate to begin sharing more personal concerns. The maturity of the group will help determine this).

III – THIRD STEP: PRAYER

Just as in the case of meditation, prayer can also have different meanings, even when there is a relationship between meditation and prayer. The third step of *Lectio Divina* is prayer. The questions that guides us now are:

How do I respond to the text?

Obviously, our response is not simply to the text as an inanimate reality, but to God who speaks to me through his Word in the Bible passage.

How do I respond to God who speaks to me in the Sacred Text?

Prayer is the first response to God. The second response would be to act in accordance with the Word of God.

Prayer may exhibit a variety of forms:

- Prayer using my own words: this may be oral (spontaneous) or written (from a prepared text).
- Some well-known corporate prayer: The Lord's Prayer, Ave Maria, Holy Rosary.
- Hymns, poems or religious songs that express the inner emotions of the disciple.
- Another Bible text as a response to the Lord.

The content of the prayer can be:

- Seeking forgiveness.
- Thanksgiving.
- Praise and blessing.
- Supplication and petition.

When *Lectio Divina* is communal we can share what the Lord has awakened in each of us, or we can propose beforehand some common sharing that involves everyone. The coordinator or leader of the prayerful reading of the Bible should prepare before hand.

Here are some examples:

- Write a prayer and present it along side a religious image.
- Distribute multiple prayers, images, Bible texts, or other material related to the subject chosen for *Lectio Divina*. Each participant would be asked to read aloud his or her material.
- Hold hands and pray together a well-known prayer.
- Have each participant light a small candle and place it in a predetermined spot.

These are the essential elements of specific prayer as the third step of *Lectio Divina*. Keep in mind, in a broader sense the entire exercise of *Lectio Divina* is prayer.

IV – FOURTH STEP: CONTEMPLATION

In the three steps already mentioned, the conscious use of our intelligence and freedom has been underscored in the analysis and appropriation of the text. In the fourth step, the effort of our intelligence or will is minimized. We are now talking about synthesizing all that was done in the earlier steps before God's presence. There are no more questions to ponder and to which we are to respond. In this step, we are in God's presence. Contemplation is the moment of inner awareness of the Word that brings together the three earlier steps. Following the difficult tasks of interpreting and applying the Word we now reach the moment when everything is placed in God's sight. This is our time to move into contemplation, remembering that contemplation in itself is a gift from God.

Can contemplation be defined? It is very difficult to define contemplation. We could call it an inner state of communion with God. For Saint Gregory the Great, contemplation consisted of the "delicious knowledge of God," where everything is impregnated with love. Contemplation is the ability to rejoice in God's light, be in God's presence, and embrace his outlook on life. It is to experience God's comfort and protection.

Contemplation is a gift that God grants to whomever he wishes, in the manner he wishes and when he wishes. For that reason, we cannot be sure that we will experience the light of God at the moment we participate in *Lectio Divina*. God will grant it as a gift when he considers it right to do so. We should not forget, however, that *Lectio Divina* is the best place for contemplation to be granted as a gift.

Throughout *Lectio Divina* there will be moments of silence when we offer ourselves, read, meditate and pray. But in the fourth step, in contemplation, silence has a special significance. It is the fundamental element to elevate our souls to God. The commitment of the participant to the Word is definitely the step of contemplation. Integral to this is an attitude of profound silence and the disposition to wait. Prayer before the exposed Sacrament or before the real presence of the Lord on the altar, are proper places for contemplation. These moments should be sought out by the participant as a personal responsibility and should be suggested by the coordinators in the communal exercises of *Lectio Divina*. A specific time of worship can be organized or a visit to a holy place with the group for prayerful reading of the Bible should be arranged.

In this step of contemplation there are no more statements to sum things up as in the earlier steps. The most important thing to keep in mind is *the need for silence, to fully 'take in' the Word.*

Some authors who write on the topic of spirituality speak of the fruits of Christian contemplation. These result from the experience of contemplation in the framework of the exercise of *Lectio Divina*. Three fruits are commonly mentioned:

1. **Experience of Consolation**: This is a profound inner happiness independent of external circumstances and independent of our internal emotional state. It is happiness of a supernatural origin, profoundly spiritual, with its beginning and end in God himself. This happiness gives one a taste for the values of the Gospel. A very clear existential desire is experienced, a desire to want to live the life of the Kingdom since it is God who orders our way forward, who stands by us, protects and cares for us.

2. **Light for Discernment**: This is the second fruit of the experience of contemplation. *To discern* in spiritual language is not a mere deductive process that considers the causes and anticipates the consequences. To discern means to make ourselves available so that the light of the Holy Spirit illuminates the soul and one is enabled to choose the best from among two good alternatives. This is not simply a moral framework, wherein the teaching of Jesus exhorts us to do good and always avoid evil. Rather, it is the ability to choose in the more complex circumstances of our contemporary life that which is the best alternative within

the Lord's will. It demands of us that we open our hearts to the action of the Spirit. This ability to discern through the Gospel is a fruit of contemplation that is available to the believer through the prayerful reading of the Bible.

3. **Strength to Sustain our Decision**: Decision follows discernment. We form decisions based upon our prayer and discernment within the framework of *Lectio Divina*. The great options of life arise before us: truth, faithfulness, righteousness, commitment. One of the fruits of contemplation is to be empowered to make right decisions, according to the Gospel, in the midst of the very real and complicated situations in life. The Holy Spirit not only illuminates the precise moment of decision, he also accompanies the believer through the consequences that result from a decision. One of the great evils of our contemporary culture is our inability to faithfully sustain over time the small or great decisions made in response to the Gospel. The gift of contemplation enables us to sustain, even in the midst of difficulties and trials along the way, the authentic options based on the Gospel that we have chosen.

V- FIFTH STEP: ACTION

In the final step of *Lectio Divina* we apply to our life what God has revealed to us through reading and meditation, and what we have made our own through prayer and contemplation. The first response to God who spoke to us in the Bible occurred in the dialogue of prayer (third step). Now, in this final step of *Lectio Divina*, we find the second response in our actions carried out in time and history.

The entire process of the prayerful reading of the Bible does not remain in the inner life of the participant, but rather it bears fruit in the daily life impregnated with the values of the Gospel. What has been read, meditated upon, prayed and contemplated must be nurtured and put into action. It needs to become part of a coherent and committed life based on the values of the Kingdom of God. Jesus said to his disciples, and among them in a special way to the Most Holy Virgin: **". . . how happy are those who hear the word of God and obey it!"** (Luke 11.28). The life of Mary and of all the Lord's disciples reflect this teaching that summarizes quite well the whole dynamic of *Lectio Divina*: Listen to God. Listen to God through his Word. Obey him by putting His Word into practice in our lives, in our daily reality.

THE WAY TO BRING THE WORD INTO OUR LIVES.

The exercise of *Lectio Divina* combines the life of prayer and the life of action for the missionary disciple. It integrates the spiritual dimension with the material; the transcendent with the historical; the eternal with the temporal. Often in the life of the Church some groups are more inclined to defend the spiritual aspect than the historical commitment and vice versa. The authentic missionary disciple balances all dimensions. The prayerful reading of the Bible knits together the most profound prayer and contemplation with daily life. The commitment and actions of daily life reflect the most religious and transcendent form of prayer and contemplation.

Our actions must be personal, according to what God puts into the heart of each participant, whether in the personal or communal experience of *Lectio Divina*. However, it may be that in some circumstances, the fruit of action from the prayerful communal reading of the Bible may prompt a unique and concrete action common to the entire group of participants. If the participants are routinely related by being in the same community, they may perceive in their dialogue with the Lord a particular need to which they feel compelled to respond. For example, the group may assume a decidedly missionary attitude with a certain sector or neighborhood of their own parish; or they may assume some kind of social or evangelistic service with an institution for the care of children or the aged. (Any such spiritual activities should be developed in conjunction with the responsible persons in the respective community to verify convenience and viability).

**"But a Samaritan who was traveling that way came upon the man,
and when he saw him, his heart was filled with pity."**
(Luke 10.33).

CONCLUSION

SOME SUGGESTIONS FOR PRACTICING *LECTIO DIVINA*

Throughout the preceding chapters, the focus has been the prayerful reading of the Bible and the steps to follow to achieve that desired goal.

Of all the various aspects discussed, three fundamentals points stand out above all else in these pages:

1. From the outset we are focused on the mystery of Scripture as the *Word of God in the language of human beings*. There is an interaction and dialogue between God and man in the Bible; humanity and God encounter one another in its writings. In Christ and from Christ, true God and true man, the living Word, we understand and find unity in Scripture.

2. The Bible is a book from the past that has *implications in the present*. In the Bible the past and the present illuminate each other. The Bible, as the written Word of God, is not a relic of the past, but the living Word of God, the eternal Word for men and women throughout history.

3. The Bible is profound and it is full of life. It depicts the interaction of God in the life of humankind. Since it is full of life, the Scriptures, read and interpreted in the Church, *give a clear orientation for our life today*.

These three aspects, which deal with the totality of Scripture, surface most in the prayerful reading of the Bible. In *Lectio Divina*, Christ as the living Word illuminates our life. The world of prayerful Bible reading becomes filled with joy when the Lord makes his Word alive in us. This is fundamental for the life of the missionary disciple, for the spiritual and evangelical life of every believer.

As we stated in the introduction, these pages are a simple manual. We should not feel bound by it. Its objective is to lead us to the Bible so that, through prayerful reading, it might become for us the Word of God that illuminates our life.

We trust in God that the biblical and spiritual springtime, achieved through the practice of *Lectio Divina*, may truly become an integral part of each of our lives. Having opened up to Christ and his Word, we must be able to say like the disciples on the road to Emmaus: **"Wasn't it like a fire burning in us when he talked to us on the road and explained the Scriptures to us?"** (Luke 24.32).

SUGGESTIONS FOR PRACTICING *LECTIO DIVINA*

Presented here are two Bible passages with guidelines and suggestions to practice the steps of *Lectio Divina*. Fundamentally, we concentrate on reading, the first step, allowing us the freedom to go deeper into the text. This is followed by meditation, prayer, contemplation and action.

FIRST EXERCISE:

God Calls Isaiah to Be a Prophet

¹In the year that King Uzziah died, I saw the Lord. He was sitting on his throne, high and exalted, and his robe filled the whole Temple. ²Around him flaming creatures were standing, each of which had six wings. Each creature covered its face with two wings, and its body with two, and used the other two for flying. ³They were calling out to each other:

"Holy, holy, holy! The Lord Almighty is holy! His glory fills the world."

⁴The sound of their voices made the foundation of the Temple shake, and the Temple itself became filled with smoke. ⁵I said, "There is no hope for me! I am doomed because every word that passes my lips is sinful, and I live among a people whose every word is sinful. And yet, with my own eyes I have seen the King, the Lord Almighty."

⁶Then one of the creatures flew down to me, carrying a burning coal that he had taken from the altar with a pair of tongs. ⁷He touched my lips with the burning coal and said, "This has touched your lips, and now your guilt is gone, and your sins are forgiven."

⁸Then I heard the Lord say, "Whom shall I send? Who will be our messenger?"

I answered, "I will go! Send me!" (Isaiah 6.1-8).

READING GUIDELINES:

From reading the text we understand that its literary genre has two principal characteristics: a vocational account and an apocalyptic reference. It is vocational in that it recounts how God called Isaiah to be his messenger. It is apocalyptic with its references to the flaming, six-winged creatures; a very high throne; the smoke; and the voice of the Lord. There is an historical reference: The death of King Uzziah (about 740 B.C.). That may not be such an important historical date in itself, but it is important in relation to the birth of the messenger in the history of the nation of Judah.

The description of the characters in the passage:

- **The narrator (Isaiah)**: Presumably, the narrator is the prophet Isaiah. The text does not state that explicitly but it is inferred in chapters 1 to 5 where reference is made to the Word of God that is revealed to the prophet. He sees the Lord and the flaming creatures, hears them and realizes that he is going to die because he has seen a vision of the Almighty Lord (cf. Exodus 33.20). He recognizes himself as a sinner who lives in the midst of a sinful people. He responds to the Lord's call and expresses his willingness to be sent out for the Lord.

- **The Lord**: He is seated upon the exalted throne and his mantle fills the temple. He asks who will go out as a messenger to fulfill his mission.

- **Flaming beings** ("seraphim"): They are six-winged creatures who cover their eyes with two wings, their bodies with two wings, and with two wings they fly. They stand around the Lord and give testament to the glory of God announcing three times that he is holy.

- **One of the beings**: He takes a burning coal from the altar to purify the narrator's mouth and then he announces that the narrator has been purged of his sins and forgiven.

With respect to the location of the incident, the only place mentioned is the temple. We are told about a very high and exalted throne. Mention is made of the altar and of the doors.

Examples of biblical memory — Jeremiah 1.4-10 and Ezekiel 2.1-15, record the vocational calls of two other Old Testament major prophets.

QUESTIONS SUGGESTED FROM THE TEXT:
- How does the text begin?
- What historical reference is mentioned?
- Who is seen in the temple?
- What characteristics does the Lord have? How is he described?
- Who appears after the description of the Lord?
- What do they do? What characteristics do they have?
- What do the flaming creatures say?
- What happens to the doors of the temple?
- What thoughts occur to Isaiah?
- Why does Isaiah think this?
- How does the prophet see himself? How does he see his people?
- What does one of the flaming creatures do?
- What does he say to Isaiah?
- What does the prophet then hear?
- Is the prophet spoken to directly or by means of a rhetorical question?
- How does Isaiah respond?

QUESTIONS SUGGESTED FOR MEDITATION:
- Am I hoping to "see" the Lord?
- Have I discovered the greatness and omnipotence of my God?
- Am I tempted to make a god of my own measure or do I really open my heart to God's transcendence?
- Do I contemplate the power and authority of God, in spite of the signs of evil

that are seen in many places in the world?

- What does it mean for me today to affirm that God is "thrice holy"?

- Have I discovered that I am weak and a sinner?

- Do I consider myself a man or woman of impure lips?

- What are the impurities on my lips today?

- Do I understand that I live with a people of unclean lips?

- What are the sins, the impurities, the detours of the people to whom I belong?

- Do I allow the Lord to purify me? Do I allow the fire of his holy glory to purify my lips?

- How do I react when the Lord tells me through his intermediaries: "your guilt is gone, and your sins are forgiven?"

- Do I allow the Lord to reconcile me? Do I allow the Lord to forgive me?

- Do I listen to God's voice? What does he say to me?

- Do I allow myself to face the questions and the proposals of the Lord?

- How do I respond?

- What meaning does the phrase, "I will go, send me" have for me today?

SUGGESTIONS FOR PRAYER:

We should read another Bible passage that illuminates the dynamic of *Lectio Divina* that we are practicing. In our text the prophet gets ready to fulfill God's will by saying: **"I will go! Send me!"** In light of this, we propose a Christological text in which we see how Jesus Christ, true God and true man, fulfills his obedience to the Father's will.

> **For this reason, when Christ was about to come into the world, he said to God: "You do not want sacrifices and offerings, but you have prepared a body for me. You are not pleased with animals burned whole on the altar or with sacrifices to take away sins. Then I said, 'Here I am, to do your will, O God, just as it is written of me in the book of the Law'"** (Hebrews 10.5-7).

Through this text we are able to relate the Mystery of Christ's obedience to the will of his Father, to our obedient response to the call of the Lord for mission. (This text in Hebrews has parallels in yet another Old Testament text - Psalm 40.6-8.)

SUGGESTIONS FOR CONTEMPLATION:

To make the Word our own, we should contemplate the greatness and transcendence of God by using the words of the seraphim in verse 3: **"Holy, holy, holy! The Lord Almighty is holy! His glory fills the world."**

We should repeat this verse quietly and in rhythm. Begin imagining the entire text and visualizing it. We should repeat the verse in our minds, repeat it with our lips, repeat it in a quiet voice, and finally in silence.

SUGGESTIONS FOR ACTION:

The response of the prophet, illuminated by Christ's submission to the will of the Father, should enable us to allow ourselves to be sent by God to fulfill his mission. The key is the verb *send* and the responsibility is to be his messenger.

On a personal level, each one should ask of themselves:

- Where does the Lord want to send me today?
- In what places does God want me to be his messenger?

Following the practice of *Lectio Divina*, we will receive the Lord's light to carry out his mission where he sends us. Here are some examples:

- The Lord sends me to be his messenger among people in my neighborhood,; among my friends; among my colleagues at work; among my classmates; among members of my sports team.

- The Lord sends me to be his messenger in more difficult situations: to places of injustice; to people suffering and abused; to areas of conflict and violence.

SECOND EXERCISE:

Jesus and Zacchaeus

¹Jesus went on into Jericho and was passing through. ²There was a chief tax collector there named Zacchaeus, who was rich. ³He was trying to see who Jesus was, but he was a little man and could not see Jesus because of the crowd. ⁴So he ran ahead of the crowd and climbed a sycamore tree to see Jesus, who was going to pass that way. ⁵When Jesus came to that place, he looked up and said to Zacchaeus, "Hurry down, Zacchaeus, because I must stay in your house today." ⁶Zacchaeus hurried down and welcomed him with great joy.

⁷All the people who saw it started grumbling, "This man has gone as a guest to the home of a sinner!"

⁸Zacchaeus stood up and said to the Lord, "Listen, sir! I will give half my belongings to the poor, and if I have cheated anyone, I will pay back four times as much." ⁹Jesus said to him, "Salvation has come to this house today, for this man, also, is a descendant of Abraham. ¹⁰The Son of Man came to seek and to save the lost" (Luke 19.1-10).

Reading Guidelines:

This incident only appears in the Gospel according to Saint Luke. Zacchaeus is the model for conversion of heart when an individual encounters Christ. A profound change, real and effective takes places in the heart of Zacchaeus when the Lord Jesus invites himself to Zacchaeus' home.

As an example of biblical memory – a similar phrase to what Jesus says in Luke 19.10: **"The Son of Man came to seek and to save the lost"** may be found in Luke 5.31-32: **Jesus answered them, "People who are well do not need a doctor, but only those who are sick. I have not come to call respectable people to repent, but outcasts."**

The places described in the account are:

- **Jericho**: A city to the southwest of Judea, near the mouth of the river Jordan. It is a very ancient city in a strategic place.

- **A tree**: A sycamore tree, similar to a fig tree, very leafy and easy to climb.

- **The home of Zacchaeus**.

The description of characters and their actions:

- **Jesus**: He enters and crosses the city; looks up and invites himself to the home of Zacchaeus; explains and proclaims what he has done with Zacchaeus; announces salvation for all who are lost.

- **Zacchaeus the Tax Collector**: He is a chief tax collector for Rome, someone with endless possibilities to become rich with ill-gotten gains. He climbs up a tree to see Jesus, but quickly descends from the tree and receives the Lord with joy. His attitude toward life changes and he willingly returns four times the money he has received by cheating others.

- **Everyone**: They criticize Jesus, displeased that he has gone to the house of a sinner.

QUESTIONS SUGGESTED FROM THE TEXT:

- What place did Jesus enter?
- What did Jesus do in the city?
- Who lived in Jericho?
- What did Zacchaeus desire?
- Why was Zacchaeus unable to see Jesus?
- What did he do? Where did he climb?
- What did Jesus do when he saw Zacchaeus up in the tree? What did he say to him?
- How did Zacchaeus react?
- What did the people say when Jesus went to Zacchaeus' home?
- What did Zacchaeus say to the Lord?
- How did Jesus respond to the words of Zacchaeus?
- Why has the Son of Man come?

QUESTIONS SUGGESTED FOR MEDITATION:

- Do I, like Zacchaeus, seek to overcome obstacles that keep me from reaching Jesus?

- Do I always realize that the Lord is seeking me and waiting for me?

- What do I do when Jesus looks into my life? What in me could move him to invite me?

- How do I respond when the Lord says to me that he wants to dwell in my house, in my life, in my heart?

- Do I react quickly and with joy?

- Do I become critical, murmuring, and do I resist accepting the truth that Jesus is compassionate and merciful toward sinners?

- Jesus enters my life and my heart: Do I allow him to transform me? Do I change my attitude for the better? Do I leave my sin to embrace a new life of grace?

- Do I seek to be generous and repair the damage done to others?

- Am I inclined to share with all, especially with those who are poor and needy, whether I have little or much?

- Do I surrender my time, my abilities and my talents to serve others?

- Do I accept salvation as God's gift for me and for all, including the worst sinners?

SUGGESTIONS FOR PRAYER:

We offer the following reflection by Pope Benedict XVI given on November 4, 2007 as a suggestion for informing our prayer:

> *Dear brothers and sisters! Today the liturgy presents for our meditation the well-known episode of Jesus' encounter with Zacchaeus in the city of Jericho. Who was Zacchaeus? A rich man who had the job of publican, that is, tax collector for the Roman authority, and precisely for that reason was considered a public sinner. When he learned that Jesus was passing through Jericho, he was moved by a great desire to see him, and since he was of short*

stature, he climbed up into a tree. Jesus stopped precisely below that tree and turned to him, calling him by name: "Zacchaeus, come down quickly; for today I must stay in your home" (Luke 19.5). What a message there is in this simple phrase! "Zacchaeus": Jesus calls by name a man who is despised by all. "Today": yes, this is for him precisely the moment of salvation. "I must stay": Why "I must"? Because the Father, rich in mercy, wants Jesus to "seek and to save that which was lost" (Luke 19.10). The grace of that unexpected encounter was such that it completely changed Zacchaeus' life: "Behold —he confessed to Jesus— I give half my goods to the poor and, if I have cheated anyone, I will restore it fourfold" (Luke 19.8). Again the Gospel tells us that love, flowing from the heart of God and acting through the heart of man, is the force that renews the world.[60]

Let the words of the Holy Father awaken in us the initial response of prayer, following the reading and meditation of Luke 19.1-10.

SUGGESTIONS FOR CONTEMPLATION:

Let us spend time contemplating the actions of Jesus when he invites himself to Zacchaeus' home. Think about this in a personal manner, as if Jesus is inviting himself to your home. Begin by recalling our Lord's words in the second part of verse 5: **"Hurry down, Zacchaeus, because I must stay in your house today."**

Substitute your own name and do not be afraid to listen to the voice of the Lord who says to us: **"Hurry down.** [*Helen, Frank, Noel, George, Patricia, Mauro. . .*]**, I want to stay in your house today."**

SUGGESTIONS FOR ACTION:

This is not a difficult text from which one might determine a personal action plan since the narrative describes a series of actions on the part of "converted" Zacchaeus. The difficulty is not in planning actions but rather in our personal conversion that must take place prior to taking positive actions. Therefore, we should propose one or two concrete steps of change and conversion in our life. They should be in relation to the negative things that we see in ourselves. Some examples:

- I will draw near to the Sacrament of Reconciliation to confess my sins and receive sacramental absolution.

- I will stop being negative and protesting about the circumstances of life.

- I will share something I value with my friends; make time to visit and give a gift to a person in need; offer a word of encouragement to someone who is suffering loneliness or depression.

- I will ask forgiveness of someone that I have offended or wounded in the past.

"…He looked up and said to Zacchaeus, "Hurry down, Zacchaeus, because I must stay in your house today."
(Luke 19.5).

MESSAGE TO THE PEOPLE OF GOD OF THE XII ORDINARY GENERAL ASSEMBLY OF THE SYNOD OF BISHOPS

Brothers and sisters,

"May God the Father and the Lord Jesus Christ grant peace, love and faith to all the brothers. May grace be with all who love our Lord Jesus Christ, in life imperishable". With this intense and passionate greeting, Saint Paul concluded his letter to the Christians of Ephesus (6.23-24). With these same words we, the Synod Fathers, gathered in Rome for the XII Ordinary General Assembly of the Synod of Bishops, under the guidance of the Holy Father Benedict XVI, open our message addressed to the vast horizon of all those who, in the various regions of the world, follow Christ as disciples, and continue to love him with an imperishable love.

We will again propose to them the voice and the light of the word of God, repeating the ancient call: "the word is very near to you, it is in your mouth and in your heart for you to put into practice" (Deuteronomy 30.14). And God himself will say to each one: "Son of man, take to heart everything I say to you, listen carefully" (Ezekiel 3.10). We are about to propose a spiritual journey consisting of four phases and that will carry us from all eternity and the infinite nature of God to our homes and the streets of our cities.

I. THE VOICE OF THE WORD: REVELATION

1. "Then the Lord spoke to you from the heart of the fire; you heard the sound of words but saw no shape; there was only a voice!" (Deuteronomy 4.12). It is Moses who speaks, evoking the experience lived by Israel in the bitter solitude of the Sinai desert. The Lord presented himself not as an image or an effigy or a statue similar to a golden calf, but with "a voice of words". It is a voice which entered the scene at the very beginning of creation, when it tore through the silence of nothingness: "In the beginning…God said, 'Let there be light,' and there was light…In the beginning was the Word: the Word was with God and the Word was God…Through him all things came into being, not one thing came into being except through him" (Genesis 1.1-3; John 1.1-3).

Creation is not born of a battle of divinities, as taught by ancient Mesopotamian myths, but of a word which defeats nothingness and creates being. The Psalmist sings: "By the word of the Lord the heavens were made, by the breath of his mouth all their array…for, the moment he spoke, it was so, no sooner had he commanded, than there it stood" (Psalm 33.6-9). And Saint Paul will repeat: God "brings the dead to life and calls into existence what does not yet exist" (Romans 4.17). Thus, a first "cosmic" revelation is found which makes creation similar to an immense page opened up before all of humanity, in which a message from the Creator can be read: "The heavens declare the glory of God, the vault of heaven proclaims his handiwork, day unto day makes known his message; night unto night hands on the knowledge. There is no speech or language where their voice is not heard. Their message goes out into all the earth" (Psalm 19.2-5).

2. The divine word is, however, also at the origin of human history. Man and woman, whom God created "in his own image" (Genesis 1.27), and who bear within themselves the divine imprint, can enter into dialogue with their Creator or can wander far from him and reject him away by sinning. The word of God, then, saves and judges, penetrating the woven fabric of history with its tales and events: "I have indeed seen the misery of my people in Egypt. I have heard them crying … I am well aware of their sufferings And I have come down to rescue them from the clutches of the Egyptians and bring them up out of that country, to a country rich and broad" (Exodus 3.7-8). The divine is therefore present in human events which, through the action of the Lord of history, are inserted in the greater plan of salvation for "everyone to be saved and reach full knowledge of the truth" (1 Timothy 2.4).

3. Consequently, the effective, creative and salvific divine word is source of being and of history, of creation and redemption. The Lord encounters humanity declaring: "I, the Lord, have spoken and done this" (Ezekiel 37.14). The voice of God then passes into the written word, the Graphé or the Graphaí, the Sacred Scriptures, as it is said in the New Testament. Moses had already descended from the mount of Sinai, "with the two tablets of the commandments in his hands, tablets inscribed on both sides, inscribed on the front and on the back. The tablets were the work of God, and the writing on them was God's writing" (Exodus 32.15-16). Moses himself obliged Israel to preserve and rewrite these "tablets of the commandments": "On these stones you must write all the words of this Law very plainly" (Deuteronomy 27.8).

The Sacred Scriptures "bear witness" to the divine word in written form. They memorialize the creative and saving event of revelation by way of canonical, historical and literary means. Therefore, the word of God precedes and goes beyond the Bible which itself is "inspired by God" and contains the efficacious divine word (cf. 2 Timothy 3.16). This is why our faith is not only centered on a book, but on a history of salvation and, as we will see, on a person, Jesus Christ, the Word of God made flesh, man and history. Precisely because the capacity of the divine word embraces and extends beyond the Scripture, the constant presence of the Holy Spirit that "will lead you to the complete truth" (John 16.13) is necessary for those who read the Bible. This is the great Tradition: the effective presence of the "Spirit of truth" in the Church, guardian of Sacred Scripture, which are authentically interpreted by the Church's *Magisterium*. This Tradition enables the Church to understand, interpret, communicate and bear witness to the word of God. Saint Paul himself, proclaiming the first Christian creed, will recognize the need to "transmit" what he "had received" from Tradition (1 Corinthians 15.3-5).

II. THE FACE OF THE WORD: JESUS CHRIST

4. In the original Greek, there are only three fundamental words: Lógos sarx eghéneto, "the Word was made flesh". And yet, this is the summit not only of that poetic and theological jewel which is the prologue to John's Gospel (John 1.14), but it is the actual heart of the Christian faith. The eternal and divine Word enters into space and time and takes on a human face and identity, so much so that it is possible to approach him directly asking, as did the group of Greeks present in Jerusalem: "We should like to see Jesus" (John 12.20-21). Words without a face are not perfect, they do not fully complete the encounter, as Job recalled, reaching the end of his dramatic itinerary of searching: "Before, I knew you only by hearsay but now"… I have "seen you with my own eyes" (Job 42.5).

Christ is "the Word [that] was with God and the Word was God" (John 1.1). "He is the image of the unseen God, the first-born of all creation" (Colossians 1.15); but he is also Jesus of Nazareth who walks the roads of a marginal province of the Roman Empire, who speaks the local language, who reveals the traits of a people, the Jews, and its culture. Therefore the real Jesus Christ is fragile and mortal flesh; he is history and humanity, but he is also glory, divinity, mystery: he who revealed God to us, the God no one has ever seen (cf. John 1.18). The Son of God continues to be so even in the dead body placed in the sepulcher and the resurrection is the living and clear proof to this fact.

5. Christian tradition has often placed the Divine Word made flesh on a parallel with the same word made book. This is what emerges already in the creed when one professes that the Son of God "was incarnate by the Holy Spirit of the Virgin Mary, and was made man", but also a profession of faith in the same "Holy Spirit, who spoke through the Prophets". The Second Vatican Council gathers this ancient tradition according to which "the body of the Son is the Scripture transmitted to us" - as Saint Ambrose affirms (In Lucam VI, 33) - and clearly declares: "For the words of God, expressed in human language, have been made like human discourse, just as the Word of the eternal Father, when he took to himself the flesh of human weakness, was in every way made like men" (DV 13).

Indeed, the Bible is also "flesh", "letter"; it expresses itself in particular languages, in literary and historical forms, in concepts tied to an ancient culture, it preserves the memories of events, often tragic; its pages not infrequently are marked by blood and violence, within it resounds the laughter of humanity and the flowing tears, as well as the cry of the distressed and the joy of those in love. For this, its "bodily" dimension requires an historical and literary analysis, which occurs through various methods and approaches offered by Biblical exegesis. Every reader of Sacred Scripture, even the most simple, must have a proportionate knowledge of the sacred text, recalling that the word is enveloped in concrete words, which is shaped and adapted to make it heard and understood by all of humanity.

This is a necessary commitment. If it is excluded, one could fall into fundamentalism which in practice denies the Incarnation of the divine Word in history, does not recognize that this word expresses itself in the Bible according to a human language, that must be decoded, studied and understood. Such an attitude ignores that divine inspiration did not erase the historical identities and personalities of its human authors. The Bible, however, is also the eternal and divine Word and for this reason requires another understanding, given by the Holy Spirit who unveils the transcendent dimension of the divine word, present in human words.

6. Here, thus, lies the necessity of the "living Tradition of all the Church" (DV 12) and of the faith to understand Sacred Scripture in a full and unified way. Should one focus only on the "letter", the Bible is only a solemn document of the past, a noble, ethical and cultural witness. If, however, the Incarnation is excluded, it could fall into a fundamentalist equivocation or a vague spiritualism or pop-psychology. Exegetical knowledge must, therefore, weave itself indissolubly with spiritual and theological tradition so that the divine and human unity of Jesus Christ and Scripture is not broken.

In this rediscovered harmony, the face of Christ will shine in its fullness and will help us to discover another unity, that profound and intimate unity of Sacred Scriptures. There are, indeed, 73 books, but they form only one "Canon", in one dialogue between God and humanity, in one plan of salvation. "At many moments in the past and by many means, God spoke to our ancestors through the prophets; but in our time, the final days, he has spoken to us in the person of his Son" (Hebrews 1.1-2). Christ thus retrospectively sheds his light on the entire development of salvation history and reveals its coherence, meaning, and direction. He is the seal, "the Alpha and the Omega" (Revelation 1.8) of a dialogue between God and his creatures distributed over time and attested to in the Bible. It is in the light of this final seal that the words of Moses and the prophets acquire their "full sense". Jesus himself had indicated this on that spring afternoon, while he made his way from Jerusalem to the town of Emmaus, dialoguing with Cleopas and his friend, explaining "to them the passages in the Scriptures that were about himself" (Luke 24.27).

That the divine Word has put on a face is at the center of Revelation. That is precisely why the ultimate finality of biblical knowledge is "not the result of an ethical choice or a lofty idea, but the encounter with an event, a person, which gives life a new horizon and a decisive direction" (*Deus caritas est*, 1).

III. THE HOUSE OF THE WORD: THE CHURCH

Just as divine wisdom in the Old Testament made her house in the cities of men and women, supporting it with seven pillars (cf. Proverbs 9.1), thus also the word of God made its house in the New Testament. The Church has as her model the mother community of Jerusalem. The Church is founded on Peter and the apostles and today, through the bishops in communion with the Successor of Peter, continues to keep, announce and interpret the word of God (cf. LG 13). In the Acts of the Apostles (2.42),

Luke traces its architecture based on four ideal pillars: "These remained faithful to the teaching of the apostles, to the brotherhood, to the breaking of bread and to the prayers".

7. Here, first of all, is the apostolic didaché, that is to say the preaching of the word of God. The Apostle Paul, in fact, warns us that "faith comes from hearing, and what is heard comes through the word of Christ" (Romans 10.17). The voice of the herald comes from the Church, which proposes kérygma, that is to say, the primary and fundamental announcement that Jesus himself had proclaimed at the beginning of his public ministry: "The time is fulfilled, and the kingdom of God is close at hand. Repent and believe the gospel" (Mark 1.15). The apostles, proclaiming the death and resurrection of Christ, announce the unveiling of the kingdom of God, that is to say, the decisive divine intervention in the history of man: "Only in him is there salvation; for of all the names in the world given to men, this is the only one by which we can be saved" (Acts 4.12). The Christian bears witness to this hope "with courtesy and respect and with a clear conscience", ready, however, to be involved and, perhaps, to be overwhelmed by the storms of refusal and persecution, knowing that "it is better to suffer doing right then for doing wrong" (1 Peter 3.16-17).

Catechesis, then, resounds in the Church: this is destined to deepen in the Christian "the understanding of the mystery of Christ in the light of God's word, so that the whole of a person's humanity is impregnated by that word" in Christianity (John Paul II, Catechesi tradendae, 20). But the high point of preaching is in the homily which, for many Christians, is still today the central moment of encounter with the word of God. In this act, the minister should be transformed into a prophet as well. He, in fact, with a clear, incisive and substantial language must not only proclaim with authority "God's wonderful works in the history of salvation" (SC 35) - offered first by a clear and vivid reading of the biblical text proposed in the liturgy - but he must also act upon it in the times and moments lived by the hearers and make the question of conversion and vital commitment blossom in their hearts: "What are we to do, brothers?" (Acts 2.37).

Preaching, catechesis and the homily therefore presuppose a reading and understanding, an explaining and interpreting, an involvement of the mind and of the heart. Thus in preaching a dual movement is achieved. With the first, one goes back to the roots of the sacred texts, the events, the first words of the history of salvation, to understand them in their meaning and in their message. With the second movement, one returns to the present, to the today lived by those who hear and read, always with Christ in mind, who is the guiding light destined to unite the Scriptures. This is what Jesus himself did - as has already been said - in his journey to Jerusalem in Emmaus with two of his disciples. This is what the deacon Phillip would do on the way from Jerusalem to Gaza, when he spoke this emblematic dialogue with the Ethiopian official: "Do you understand what you are reading? ... How could I, unless I have someone to guide me?" (Acts 8.30-31). And the finality will be the full encounter with Christ in the sacrament. This is how the second pillar that supports the Church, the house of the divine word, presents itself.

8. It is the breaking of the bread. The scene at Emmaus (cf. Luke 24.13-35) is once again exemplary, and reproduces what happens every day in our churches: the homily by Jesus about Moses and the prophets gives way to the breaking of the Eucharistic Bread at the table. This is the moment of God's intimate dialogue with His people. It is the act of the new covenant sealed in the blood of Christ (cf. Luke 22.20). It is the supreme work of the Word who offers himself as food in his immolated body, it is the source and summit of the life and mission of the Church. The Gospel account of the Last Supper, the memorial of Christ's sacrifice, when proclaimed in the eucharistic celebration, through the invocation of the Holy Spirit, becomes event and sacrament. This is why the Second Vatican Council, in a very intense passage, declared: "The Church has always venerated the divine Scriptures just as she venerates the body of the Lord, since, especially in the sacred liturgy, she unceasingly receives and offers to the faithful the bread of life from the table both of God's word and of Christ's body" (DV 21). Therefore, we must place at the center of Christian life "the liturgy of the word and the eucharistic liturgy, [which] are so closely connected with each other that they form but one single act of worship" (SC 56).

9. The third pillar of the spiritual building of the Church, the house of the word, is made up of prayers, woven from - as recalled by Saint Paul - "psalms and hymns and inspired songs" (Colossians 3.16). A privileged place is naturally taken by the Liturgy of the Hours, the prayer of the Church par excellence, destined to give rhythm to the days and times of the Christian year, offering, above all with the Psalmody, the daily spiritual food of the faithful. Alongside this and the community celebrations of the

word, tradition has introduced the practice of *Lectio Divina*, the prayerful reading in the Holy Spirit that is able to open to the faithful the treasure of the word of God, and also to create the encounter with Christ, the living divine Word.

This begins with the reading (*lectio*) of the text, which provokes the question of true knowledge of its real content: what does the biblical text say in itself? Then follows meditation (*meditatio*) where the question is: what does the Biblical text say to us? In this manner, one arrives at prayer (*oratio*), which presupposes this other question: what do we say to the Lord in answer to his word? And one ends with contemplation (*contemplatio*) during which we assume, as God's gift, the same gaze in judging reality and ask ourselves: what conversion of the mind, the heart and life does the Lord ask of us?

Before the prayerful reader of the word of God rises ideally the figure of Mary, the Mother of the Lord, who "treasured all these things and pondered them in her heart" (Luke 2.19; cf. 2.51), that is - as the original Greek says - finding the profound knot that unites apparently distinct events, acts and things in the great divine plan. The attitude of Mary, the sister of Martha can also be proposed to the faithful, when they read the Bible, because she sits at the feet of the Lord listening to his word, not allowing external concerns to absorb her soul completely, allowing even the free time for "the better part" which must not be taken away (cf. Luke 10.38-42).

10. Finally, we reach the last pillar that supports the Church, the house of the word: the *koinonía*, brotherly love, another name for the *agápe*, that is to say, Christian love. As Jesus mentioned, to become his brothers and his sisters one must be like "those who hear the word of God and put it into practice" (Luke 8.21). Authentic hearing is obeying and acting. It means making justice and love blossom in life. It is offering, in life and in society, a witness like the call of the prophets, which continuously united the word of God and life, faith and rectitude, worship and social commitment. This is what Jesus stated many times, beginning with the famous warning in the Sermon on the Mount: "It is not anyone who says to me, 'Lord, Lord', who will enter the kingdom of Heaven, but the person who does the will of my Father in heaven" (Matthew 7.21). This phrase seems to echo the divine word proposed by Isaiah: "this people approaches me only in words, honors me only with lip-service, while their hearts are far from me" (29.13). These warnings also concern the churches when they are not faithful to the obedient hearing of the word of God.

Therefore this must already be visible and legible on the face and in the hands of the faithful, as suggested by Saint Gregory the Great who saw in Saint Benedict, and in other great men of God, witnesses of communion with God and with the sisters and brothers, the word of God come to life. The just and faithful man not only "explains" the Scriptures, but also "unfolds" them before all as a living and practiced reality. This is why *viva lectio, vita bonorum*, the life of the good is a living lecture/lesson of the word of God. Saint John Chrysostom had already observed that the apostles came down from the mount in Galilee, where they had met the risen Lord, without any written stone tablets as Moses had: their lives would become the living gospel, from that moment on.

In the house of the word we also encounter brothers and sisters from other Churches and ecclesial communities who, even with the still existing separations, find themselves with us in the veneration and love for the word of God, the principle and source of a first and real unity, even if not a full unity. This bond must always be reinforced through the common biblical translations, the spreading of the sacred text, ecumenical biblical prayer, exegetical dialogue, the study and the comparison between the various interpretations of the Holy Scriptures, the exchange of values inherent in the various spiritual traditions and the announcement and the common witness of the word of God in a secularized world.

IV. THE ROADS OF THE WORD: MISSION

"For the Law will go forth from Zion and the word of the Lord from Jerusalem" (Isaiah 2.3). The embodied Word of God "issues from" his house, the temple, and walks along the roads of the world to encounter the great pilgrimage that the people of earth have taken up in search of truth, justice and peace. In fact, even in the modern secularized city, in its squares and in its streets - where disbelief and indifference seem to reign, where evil seems to prevail over good, creating the impression of a victory of Babylon over Jerusalem - one can find a hidden yearning, a germinating hope, a quiver of expectation. As can be read in the book of the prophet Amos, "The days are coming, declares the Lord God, when I shall send a famine on the country: not hunger for food, not thirst for water, but famine for hearing the word of the Lord" (8:11). The evangelizing mission of the Church wants to answer this hunger.. Even the risen Christ makes an appeal to the hesitant apostles, to go forth from their protected horizon: "Go, therefore, and make disciples of all nations…and teach them to observe the commands I gave you" (Matthew 28.19-20). The Bible is fraught with appeals "not to be silent", to "speak out", to "proclaim the word at the right and at the wrong time", to be the sentinels that tear away the silence of indifference. The roads that open before us are not only the ones upon which Saint Paul and the first evangelizers traveled but are also the ones of all the missionaries who, after them, go towards the people in faraway lands.

11. Communication now casts a network that envelops the entire globe and the call of Christ gains a new meaning: "What I say to you in the dark, tell in the daylight, what you hear in whispers, proclaim from the housetops" (Matthew 10.27). Of course, the sacred word must have its primary transparency and diffusion through the printed text, with translations made according to the multiplicity of languages on our planet. But the voice of the divine word must echo even through the radio, the information highway of the internet, the channels of "on line" virtual circulation, CDs, DVDs, podcasts, etc. It must appear on all television and movie screens, in the press, and in cultural and social events.

This new communication, in relationship to the traditional one, has created its own specific and expressive grammar and, therefore, makes it necessary not only to be technically prepared, but also culturally prepared for this task. In an age of images particularly provided by the dominating means of communication, such as television, the privileged model of Christ is still meaningful and evocative today. He would turn to the sign, the story, the example, the daily experience, the parable: "He told them many things in parables … indeed, he would never speak to them except in parables" (Matthew 13.3-34). In proclaiming the kingdom of God, Jesus never spoke over the heads of the people with a vague, abstract or ethereal language. Rather, he would conquer them by starting there where their feet were placed, in order to lead them, through daily events, to the revelation of the kingdom of heaven. Thus, the scene evoked by John becomes significant: "Some wanted to arrest him, but no one actually laid a hand on him. The guards went back to the chief priests and Pharisees who said to them, 'Why haven't you brought him?' The guards replied, 'No one has ever spoken like this man'"(7.44-46).

12. Christ proceeds along the streets of our cities and stops at the doorstep of our homes: "Look, I am standing at the door, knocking. If one of you hears me calling

and opens the door, I will come in to share a meal at that person's side" (Revelation 3.20). The family, enclosed between the domestic walls with its joys and sufferings, is a fundamental space where the word of God is to be allowed to enter. The Bible is full of small and great family stories, and the Psalmist depicts with liveliness the serene picture of a father sitting at the table, surrounded by his wife, like a fruitful vine, and by his children, "shoots of an olive tree" (Psalm 128). In the same way, Christianity itself, from its origins, celebrated the liturgy in the daily home life, just as Israel entrusted the Passover celebration to the family (cf. Exodus 12.21-27). The spreading of the word of God is passed on through the generations so that parents become "the first preachers of the faith" (LG 11). Once more the Psalmist recalled that: "What we have heard and know, what our ancestors have told us, we shall not conceal from their descendants, but will tell to a generation still to come: the praises of the Lord, his power, the wonderful deeds he has done ... They should be sure to tell their own children" (Psalm 78.3-4, 6).

Therefore, every home should have its own Bible and safeguard it in a visible and dignified way, to read it and to pray with it, while, at the same time, the family should propose forms and models of a prayerful, catechetical and didactic education on how to use the Scriptures, so that "young men and women, old people and children together" (Psalm 148.12) may hear, understand, glorify and live the word of God. In particular, the new generations, children and youth, should be the ones receiving an appropriate and specific pedagogy that leads them to experience the fascination of the figure of Christ, opening the door of their mind and their heart, as well as through the encounter with and authentic witness of adults, the positive influence of friends and the great company of the ecclesial community.

13. Jesus, in his parable of the sower, reminds us that there are arid lands, full of rocks, choked by thorns (cf. Matthew 13.3-7). He who goes forth into the streets of the world also discovers the slums where suffering and poverty, humiliation and oppression, marginalization and misery, physical and psychological ills and loneliness can be found. Often the stones on the road are bloody because of wars and violence; in the palaces of power, corruption meets injustice. The voices of the persecuted rise on behalf of faithfulness to their conscience and fidelity to their faith. One can be swept away by the crises of life, or a soul can be devoid of any meaning that would give sense and value to life itself. Like "phantoms who go their way, mere vapor their pursuits"

(Psalm 39.7), many feel the silence of God, his apparent absence and indifference, hanging over them: "How long, Lord, will you forget me? For ever? How long will you turn away your face from me?" (Psalm 13.1). And, in the end, there arises for everyone, the mystery of death.

This immense sigh of suffering that rises from the earth to heaven is continuously represented by the Bible, which proposes an historical and incarnated faith. It is enough to think only of the pages marked by violence and oppression, of the harsh and continuous cry of Job, of the vehement pleas of the Psalms, of the subtle internal crisis that passes through the soul of Qoheleth, of the vigorous prophetic denunciations against social injustice. The sentence of the radical sin that appears in all its devastating force, from the beginning of humanity in a fundamental text of Genesis (chapter 3), is unconditional. In fact, the "mystery of iniquity" is present and acts in history, but it is revealed by the word of God that assures the victory of good over evil, in Christ.

But above all in the Scriptures, the figure of Christ, who begins his public ministry with a proclamation of hope for the last persons of the earth, dominates: "The spirit of the Lord is upon me, for he has anointed me to bring the good news to the afflicted. He has sent me to proclaim liberty to captives, sight to the blind, to let the oppressed go free, to proclaim a year of favour from the Lord" (Luke 4.18-19). He repeatedly places his hands on ill and diseased flesh. His words proclaim justice, instill courage to the disheartened and offer forgiveness to sinners. Finally, he himself approaches the lowest level, "he emptied himself" of his glory , "taking the form of a slave, becoming as human beings are; and being in every way like a human being, he was humbler yet, even to accepting death, death on a cross" (Philippians 2.7-8). In this way Christ feels the fear of death ("'Father', he said, 'if you are willing, take this cup away from me'"), He experiences loneliness because of the abandonment and betrayal by friends, he penetrates the darkness of the cruelest physical pain through his crucifixion and even the darkness of the Father's silence ("My God, my God, why have you forsaken me?") (Mark 15.34) and reaches the last abyss of any man, that of death ("he gave a loud cry and breathed his last"). To him, the definition that Isaiah gave to the servant of the Lord truly can be applied: "the lowest of men, a man of sorrows" (53.3).

Even so, even in that extreme moment, he does not cease being the Son of God: in his solidarity of love and with the sacrifice of himself, he sows a seed of divinity in the finiteness and evil of humanity, in other words, a principle of freedom and salvation. With his offering of himself to us he pours out redemption on pain and death, assumed and lived by him, and also opens to us the dawn of resurrection. Therefore the Christian has the mission to announce this divine word of hope, by sharing with the poor and the suffering, through the witness of his faith in the kingdom of truth and life, of holiness and grace, of justice, of love and peace, through the loving closeness that neither judges nor condemns, but that sustains, illuminates, comforts and forgives, following the words of Christ: "Come to me, all you who labour and are overburdened, and I will give you rest" (Matthew 11.28).

14. Along the roads of the world, the divine word generates for us Christians an equally intense encounter with the Jewish people, who are intimately bound through the common recognition and love for the Scripture of the Old Testament and because from Israel "so far as physical descent is concerned, came Christ" (Romans 9.5). Every page of the Jewish Scriptures enlighten the mystery of God and of man. They are treasures of reflection and morality, an outline of the long itinerary of the history of salvation to its integral fulfillment, and illustrate with vigor the incarnation of the divine word in human events. They allow us to fully understand the figure of Christ, who declared "Do not imagine that I have come to abolish the Law or the Prophets. I have come not to abolish but to fulfill them" (Matthew 5.17). These are a way of dialogue with the chosen people, "who were adopted as children, the glory was theirs and the covenants; to them were given the Law and the worship of God and the promises" (Romans 9.4), and they allow us to enrich our interpretation of the Sacred Scriptures with the fruitful resources of the Hebrew exegetical tradition.

"Blessed be my people Egypt, Assyria my creation, and Israel my heritage" (Isaiah 19.25). The Lord, then, spreads the protective mantle of his blessing all over the peoples of the earth: "he wants everyone to be saved and reach full knowledge of the truth" (1 Timothy 2.4). We, also as Christians are invited, along the roads of the world - without falling into a syncretism that confuses and humiliates our own spiritual identity, to enter into dialogue with respect towards men and women of the other religions, who faithfully hear and practice the directives of their sacred books, starting with Islam, which welcomes many biblical figures, symbols and themes in its tradition, and which offers the witness of sincere faith in the One, compassionate and merciful God, the Creator of all beings and Judge of humanity.

The Christian also finds common harmony with the great religious traditions of the Orient that teach us, in their holy writings, respect for life, contemplation, silence, simplicity, renunciation, as occurs in Buddhism. Or, as in Hinduism, they exalt the sense of the sacred, sacrifice, pilgrimage, fasting, and sacred symbols. Or, as in Confucianism, they teach wisdom and family and social values. Even to the traditional religions with their spiritual values expressed in the rites and oral cultures, we would like to pay our cordial attention and engage in a respectful dialogue with them. Also to those who do not believe in God but who endeavour to "do what is right, to love goodness and to walk humbly" (Micah 6.8), we must work with them for a more just and peaceful world, and offer in dialogue our genuine witness to the Word of God that can reveal to them new and higher horizons of truth and love.

15. In his *Letter to the Artists* (1999), John Paul II recalled that "Sacred Scripture has thus become a sort of 'immense vocabulary' (Paul Claudel) and 'iconographic atlas' (Marc Chagall), from which both Christian culture and art have drawn" (No. 5). Goethe was convinced that the Gospel was the "mother tongue of Europe". The Bible, as it is commonly said, is "the great code" of universal culture: artists imaginatively dipped their paintbrush in that alphabet coloured by stories, symbols, and figures which are the biblical pages. Musicians composed their harmonies around the sacred texts, especially the Psalms. For centuries authors went back to those old stories that became existential parables; poets asked themselves about the mystery of the spirit, infinity, evil, love, death and life, frequently gathering the poetical feelings that enlivened the biblical pages. Thinkers, men of learning and society itself frequently used the spiritual and ethical concepts (for example the Decalogue) of the word of God as a reference, even if merely in contrast. Even when the figure or the idea present in the Scriptures was deformed, it was recognized as being an essential and constitutive element of our civilization.

Because of this, the Bible - which teaches us also the via pulchritudinis, that is to say, the path of beauty to understand and reach God (as Psalm 47.7 invites us: "learn the music, let it sound for God!") - is necessary not only for the believer, but for all to rediscover the authentic meanings of various cultural expressions and above all to find our historical, civil, human and spiritual identity once again. This is the origin of our greatness and through it we can present ourselves with our noble heritage to other civilizations and cultures, without any inferiority complex. The Bible should, therefore, be known and studied by all, under this extraordinary profile of beauty and human and cultural fruitfulness.

Nevertheless, the word of God - using a meaningful Pauline image – "cannot be chained up" (2 Timothy 2.9) to a culture; on the contrary, it aspires to cross borders and the Apostle himself was an exceptional craftsman of inculturation of the biblical message into new cultural references. This is what the Church is called upon to perform even today through a delicate but necessary process, which received a strong impulse from the *Magisterium* of Pope Benedict XVI. She should make the word of God penetrate into the many cultures and express it according to their languages, their concepts, their symbols and their religious traditions. But she should always be able to maintain the genuine substance of its contents, watching over and controlling the risks of degeneration.

Therefore the Church must make the values that the word of God offers to all cultures shine, so they may be purified and fruitful. As John Paul II said to the Bishops of Kenya during his trip to Africa in 1980, "inculturation will truly be a reflection of the Incarnation of the Word, when a culture, transformed and regenerated by the gospel, brings forth from its own living tradition original expressions of Christian life, celebration and thought."

CONCLUSION

"Then I heard the voice I had heard from heaven speaking to me again. 'Go', it said, 'and take that open scroll from the hand of the angel standing on sea and land'. I went to the angel and asked him to give me the small scroll, and he said, 'Take it and eat it; it will turn your stomach sour, but it will taste as sweet as honey'. So I took it out of the angel's hand, and I ate it and it tasted sweet as honey, but when I had eaten it my stomach turned sour" (Revelation 10.8-11).

Brothers and sisters of the whole world, let us receive this invitation; let us approach the table of the word of God, so as to be nourished and live "not on bread alone but on every word that comes from the mouth of God" (Deuteronomy 8.3; Matthew 4.4). Sacred Scripture - as affirmed by a great figure of the Christian culture – "has provided passages of consolation and of warning for all conditions" (B. Pascal, Pensées, no. 532 ed. Brunschvicg).

The word of God, in fact, is "sweeter than honey, that drips from the comb" (Psalm 19.10), "Your word is a lamp for my feet, a light on my path" (Psalm 119.105), but is also: "like fire, says the Lord, like a hammer shattering a rock" (Jeremiah 23.29). It is like the rain that irrigates the earth, fertilizes it and makes it spring forth, and in doing this he makes the aridity of our spiritual deserts flourish (cf. Isaiah 55.10-11). But it is also: "something alive and active: it cuts more incisively than any two-edged sword: it can seek out the place where soul is divided from spirit, or joints from marrow; it can pass judgment on secret emotions and thoughts" (Hebrews 4.12).

Our gaze is turned lovingly towards all those engaged in study, catechists and the other servants of the word of God to express our most intense and cordial gratitude for their precious and important ministry. We also address our persecuted brothers and sisters or those who are put to death because of the word of God and because of the witness they render to the Lord Jesus (cf. Revelation 6.9): as witnesses and martyrs they tell us of "the power of the word" (Romans 1.16), origin of their faith, of their hope and of their love for God and for men.

Let us now remain silent, to hear the word of God with effectiveness and let us maintain this silence after hearing, so that it may continue to dwell in us, to live in us, and to speak to us. Let it resonate at the beginning of our day so that God has the first word and let it echo in us in the evening so that God has the last word.

Dear brothers and sisters, "All those who are with me send their greetings. Greetings to those who love us in the faith. Grace be with you all!" (Titus 3.15).

ENDNOTES

Chapter 1

[1] His Holiness Pope Paul V1 promulgated Dogmatic Constitution on Divine Revelation, *Dei Verbum* 9a (November 18, 1965) - http://www.vatican.va/archive/hist_councils/ii_vatican_council/documents/vat-ii_const_19651118_dei-verbum_en.html.

[2] His Holiness Pope Benedict XVI, Message to the People of God of the XII Ordinary General Assembly of the Synod of Bishops, (October, 2008) - http://www.vatican.va/roman_curia/synod/documents/rc_synod_doc_20081024_message-synod_en.html.

[3] *Dei Verbum* 12a.

[4] Ibid. 13.

[5] Ibid. 11a.

[6] Catechism of the Catholic Church, Part One, Section One, Chapter Two, Article 3 - Inspiration and Truth of Sacred Scripture 107, http://www.vatican.va/archive/ccc_css/archive/catechism/p1s1c2a3.htm#II. Also refer to *Dei Verbum* 11.

[7] St. Augustine, *Homilies on the Gospel of John* 1.1, (New City Press: New York, 2009).

Chapter 2

[8] *Dei Verbum* 10a.

[9] His Holiness Pope Benedict XVI, Message to the People of God of the XII Ordinary General Assembly of the Synod of Bishops, (October, 2008) - http://www.vatican.va/roman_curia/synod/documents/rc_synod_doc_20081024_message-synod_en.html.

[10] Cf. *Dei Verbum* 10

[11] His Holiness Pope Benedict XVI, Message to the People of God of the XII Ordinary General Assembly of the Synod of Bishops, (October, 2008) - http://www.vatican.va/roman_curia/synod/documents/rc_synod_doc_20081024_message-synod_en.html.

[12] Cf. *Dei Verbum*, 10b.

[13] *Dei Verbum* 12c.

[14] *Dei Verbum* 11b.

[15] Ibid. 10c.

[16] Ibid. 12c. Also refer to Catechism of the Catholic Church, Part One, Section One, Chapter Two, Article 3 - Inspiration and Truth of Sacred Scripture 111, http://www.vatican.va/archive/ccc_css/archive/catechism/p1s1c2a3.htm#II.

[17] Cf. *Dei Verbum*, 11.

[18] Cf. *Dei Verbum*, 12.

[19] XII Ordinary General Assembly of the Synod of Bishops, Final List of Propositions, Part 1. 5, (October, 2008). The link is for the Italian version. http://www.vatican.va/roman_curia/synod/documents/rc_synod_doc_20081025_elenco-prop-finali_it.html#Spirito_Santo_e_Parola_di_Dio.

[20] His Holiness Pope Benedict XVI, Message to the People of God of the XII Ordinary General Assembly of the Synod of Bishops 5c, (October, 2008) - http://www.vatican.va/roman_curia/synod/documents/rc_synod_doc_20081024_message-synod_en.html.

[21] *Dei Verbum* 12b.

Chapter 3

[22] R.G. Jenkins, "The Biblical Text of the Commentaries of Eusebius and Jerome on Isaiah," *Abr-nahrain*. Leiden, 22 (1983/84), pp. 64-78.

[23] Blaise Pascal, *Thoughts,* Section XII - Proofs of Jesus Christ, translated by W. F. Trotter. Vol. XLVIII, Part 1. The Harvard Classics. (New York: P.F. Collier & Son, 1909–14).

[24] Council of Trent, Session XXII, *Doctrine on the Holy Sacrifice of the Mass*, c. 2.

[25] Cf. St. Augustine, *Tractatus in Ioannem*, VI, n. 7.

[26] His Holiness Pope Paul V1 promulgated Constitution on the Sacred Liturgy – *Sacrosanctum Concilium*, (December 4, 1963). http://www.vatican.va/archive/hist_councils/ii_vatican_council/documents/vat-ii_const_19631204_sacrosanctum-concilium_en.html.

[27] "In" and "for" man: cf. Heb. 1, and 4, 7; ("in"): 2 Sm. 23,2; Matt.1:22 and various places; ("for"): First Vatican Council, Schema on Catholic Doctrine, note 9: Coll. Lac. VII, 522.

[28] *Dei Verbum* 4a.

[29] Sidney H. Griffith, *'Faith Adoring the Mystery': Reading the Bible with St. Ephrem the Syrian*, (Marquette University Press, Milwaukee, 1997), pp. iv.

[30] His Holiness Pope Benedict XVI, Message to the People of God of the XII Ordinary General Assembly of the Synod of Bishops, I. 4, (October, 2008) - http://www.vatican.va/roman_curia/synod/documents/rc_synod_doc_20081024_message-synod_en.html.

[31] His Holiness John Paul II, Post Synodal Exhortation – *Ecclesia in America* 67. http://www.vatican.va/holy_father/john_paul_ii/apost_exhortations/documents/hf_jp-ii_exh_22011999_ecclesia-in-america_en.html. Also refer to *Aparecida 2007, Luces Para América Latina*, (Librería Editrice Vaticana, 2008), 107 and 392.

[32] St. Augustine, "Quest. in Hept." 2,73: *PL* 34,623.

[33] St. Irenaeus, *Against Heretics*, III, 21,3: *PG* 7,950. St. Cyril of Jerusalem, *Mystagogical Catechesis*, 4,35; *PG* 33,497. Theodore of Mopsuestia, *In Sophia*, 1,4-6: *PG* 66, 452D-453A.

[34] *Dei Verbum* 16.

[35] *Compendium of the Catechism of the Catholic Church*, (Librería Editrice Vaticana, 2005), 22. http://www.vatican.va/archive/compendium_ccc/documents/archive_2005_compendium-ccc_en.html.

Chapter 4

[36] His Holiness John Paul II, Apostolic Letter – *Novo Millennio Ineunte*, (2000), 30, 31. http://www.vatican.va/holy_father/john_paul_ii/apost_letters/documents/hf_jp-ii_apl_20010106_novo-millennio-ineunte_en.html.

[37] His Holiness Pope Benedict XVI, Encyclical Letter - *Deus Caritas Est,* 1b. http://www.vatican.va/holy_father/benedict_xvi/encyclicals/documents/hf_ben-xvi_enc_20051225_deus-caritas-est_en.html.

[38] *Aparecida* 244.

[39] St. Maximus the Confessor, *Questions to Thalassius*, *PG*, vol. 90.

[40] *Deus Caritas Est,* 41.

[41] *Aparecida* 266.

[42] His Holiness Benedict XVI, *Angelus en Pompeii*, (October 19, 2008). http://www.vatican.va/holy_father/benedict_xvi/angelus/2008/documents/hf_ben-xvi_ang_20081019_pompei_en.html.

[43] His Holiness Pope Benedict XVI , Synod on the Word of God, *Propositio n. 55*

Chapter 5

[44] Guigo II, *Scala Claustralium*. Also refer to *The Ladder of Monks*, trans. Edmund Colledge and James Walsh, (New York: Double Day, 1978).

[45] St. John Chrysostom, *Homilies on St. Matthew*, II.

[46] *Dei Verbum* 25a.

[47] *Propositio* 32.

[48] Cf. His Holiness John Paul II, Apostolic Letter *Dies Domini* (May 31, 1998), 40: *AAS* 90 (1998), 738.

[49] *Ecclesia in America* 31.

[50] *Novo Millennio Ineunte*, 39.

[51] *Cf. Dei Verbum 25*.

[52] His Holiness Pope Benedict XVI , Address to the International Congress to commemorate the 40th anniversary of *Dei Verbum*, Castel Gandolfo, (September 2005). http://www.vatican.va/holy_father/benedict_xvi/speeches/2005/september/documents/hf_ben-xvi_spe_20050916_40-dei-verbum_en.html.

[53] His Holiness Pope Benedict XVI, Reflection at the First General Congregation for the XI Ordinary General Assembly of the Synod of Bishops, (2 – 23 October, 2005). http://www.vatican.va/news_services/press/sinodo/documents/bollettino_21_xi-ordinaria-2005/02_inglese/b05_02.html.

[54] His Holiness Pope Benedict XVI, *Angelus*, (6 November, 2005). http://www.vatican.va/holy_father/benedict_xvi/angelus/2005/documents/hf_ben-xvi_ang_20051106_en.html.

[55] His Holiness Pope Benedict XVI, Message on the Occasion of the 21st World Youth Day, (9 April, 2006). http://www.vatican.va/holy_father/benedict_xvi/messages/youth/documents/hf_ben-xvi_mes_20060222_youth_en.html.

[56] *Aparecida* 249.

[57] Cardinal Carlos Maria Martini, *A People on the Pathway*, pp. 13. Also refer to *Lectio Divina - Ora et Labora* 35, (1980), pp. 51-55.

[58] Bernardo Olivera, *Monastic Notebooks* 57, pp. 181. Also refer to La Tradición de la *Lectio Divina*, - *Cuadernos Monásticos* 16, (1981), pp. 179-203; fr: *La Vie Spirituelle* 76, (1996), 720, pp. 361-369.

Conclusion

[59] Pontifical Biblical Commission, "The Interpretation of the Bible in the Church," IV.C.2 (April 23, 1993). http://catholic-resources.org/ChurchDocs/PBC_Interp.html.

[60] His Holiness Benedict XVI, Angelus, (November 4, 2007). http://www.vatican.va/holy_father/benedict_xvi/angelus/2007/documents/hf_ben-xvi_ang_20071104_en.html.

BIBLIOGRAPHY

His Holiness Pope Benedict XVI, Message to the People of God of the XII Ordinary General Assembly of the Synod of Bishops, (October, 2008) - http://www.vatican.va/roman_curia/synod/documents/rc_synod_doc_20081024_message-synod_en.html.

Angelus en Pompeii, (October 19, 2008). http://www.vatican.va/holy_father/benedict_xvi/angelus/2008/documents/hf_ben-xvi_ang_20081019_pompei_en.html.

Angelus, (November 4, 2007). http://www.vatican.va/holy_father/benedict_xvi/angelus/2007/documents/hf_ben-xvi_ang_20071104_en.html.

Message on the Occasion of the 21st World Youth Day, (9 April, 2006). http://www.vatican.va/holy_father/benedict_xvi/messages/youth/documents/hf_ben-xvi_mes_20060222_youth_en.html.

Angelus, (6 November, 2005). http://www.vatican.va/holy_father/benedict_xvi/angelus/2005/documents/hf_ben-xvi_ang_20051106_en.html.

Reflection at the First General Congregation for the XI Ordinary General Assembly of the Synod of Bishops, (2 – 23 October, 2005). http://www.vatican.va/news_services/press/sinodo/documents/bollettino_21_xi-ordinaria-2005/02_inglese/b05_02.html.

Address to the International Congress to commemorate the 40th anniversary of *Dei Verbum*, Castel Gandolfo, (September 2005). http://www.vatican.va/holy_father/benedict_xvi/speeches/2005/september/documents/hf_ben-xvi_spe_20050916_40-dei-verbum_en.html.

Encyclical Letter - *Deus Caritas Est*, 1b. http://www.vatican.va/holy_father/benedict_xvi/encyclicals/documents/hf_ben-xvi_enc_20051225_deus-caritas-est_en.html.

Synod on the Word of God, *Propositio n. 55*

His Holiness Pope John Paul II, Post Synodal Exhortation – *Ecclesia in America*. http://www.vatican.va/holy_father/john_paul_ii/apost_exhortations/documents/hf_jp-ii_exh_22011999_ecclesia-in-america_en.html.

Apostolic Letter *Dies Domini* (May 31, 1998), 40: *AAS* 90 (1998).

Apostolic Letter – *Novo Millennio Ineunte*, (2000). http://www.vatican.va/holy_father/john_paul_ii/apost_letters/documents/hf_jp-ii_apl_20010106_novo-millennio-ineunte_en.html.

His Holiness Pope Paul V1 promulgated Constitution on the Sacred Liturgy – *Sacrosanctum Concilium*, (December 4, 1963). http://www.vatican.va/archive/hist_councils/ii_vatican_council/documents/vat-ii_const_19631204_sacrosanctum-concilium_en.html.

Dogmatic Constitution on Divine Revelation, *Dei Verbum* (November 18, 1965) -http://www.vatican.va/archive/hist_councils/ii_vatican_council/documents/vat-ii_const_19651118_dei-verbum_en.html.

XII Ordinary General Assembly of the Synod of Bishops, Final List of Propositions, Part 1. 5, (October, 2008). http://www.vatican.va/roman_curia/synod/documents/rc_synod_doc_20081025_elenco-prop-finali_it.html#Spirito_Santo_e_Parola_di_Dio.

Council of Trent, Session XXII, *Doctrine on the Holy Sacrifice of the Mass*, c. 2.

Compendium of the Catechism of the Catholic Church, (Librería Editrice Vaticana, 2005). http://www.vatican.va/archive/compendium_ccc/documents/archive_2005_compendium-ccc_en.html.

Pontifical Biblical Commission, "The Interpretation of the Bible in the Church," IV.C.2 (April 23, 1993).

http://catholic-resources.org/ChurchDocs/PBC_Interp.html.

Catechism of the Catholic Church, Part One, Section One, Chapter Two, Article 3 - Inspiration and Truth of Sacred Scripture 107, http://www.vatican.va/archive/ccc_css/archive/catechism/p1s1c2a3.htm#II.

Aparecida 2007, Luces Para América Latina, (Librería Editrice Vaticana, 2008), 107 and 392.

St. Augustine, *Tractatus in Ioannem*, VI, n. 7.
"Quest. in Hept." 2,73: *PL* 34,623.
Homilies on the Gospel of John 1.1, (New City Press: New York, 2009).

St. Cyril of Jerusalem, *Mystagogical Catechesis*, 4,35; *PG* 33.

St. Irenaeus, *Against Heretics*, III, 21,3: *PG* 7.

St. John Chrysostom, *Homilies on St. Matthew*, II.

St. Maximus the Confessor, *Questions to Thalassius*, *PG*, vol. 90.

Theodore of Mopsuestia, *In Sophia*, 1,4-6: *PG* 66.

Colledge, Edmund and Walsh, James trans., *The Ladder of Monks*, (New York: Double Day, 1978).

Griffith, Sidney H., *'Faith Adoring the Mystery': Reading the Bible with St. Ephrem the Syrian*, (Marquette University Press, Milwaukee, 1997).

Guigo II, *Scala Claustralium*.

Jenkins, R.G., "The Biblical Text of the Commentaries of Eusebius and Jerome on Isaiah," *Abr-nahrain*. Leiden, 22 (1983/84).

Martini, Carlos Maria Cardinal, *A People on the Pathway*.
Lectio Divina - Ora et Labora 35, (1980).

Olivera, Bernardo, *Monastic Notebooks* 57.

La Tradición de la *Lectio Divina*, - *Cuadernos Monásticos* 16, (1981), fr: *La Vie Spirituelle* 76, (1996).

Pascal, Blaise, *Thoughts,* Section XII – Proofs of Jesus Christ, translated by W. F. Trotter. Vol. XLVIII, Part 1, The Harvard Classics, (New York: P.F. Collier & Son, 1909–14).

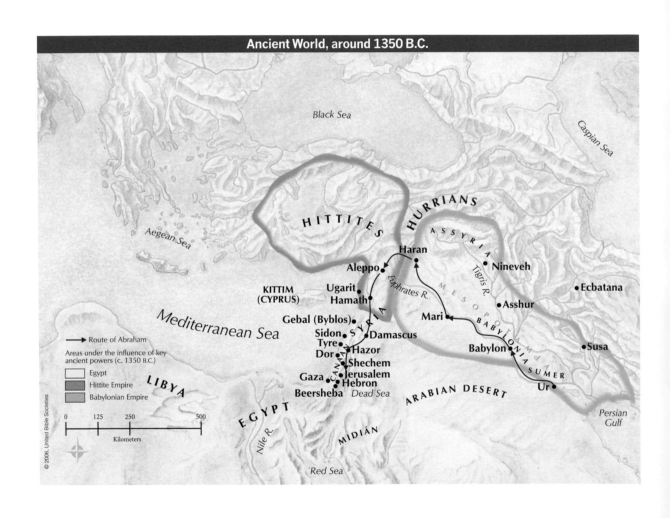

Ancient World, around 1350 B.C.

Black Sea

Caspian Sea

Aegean Sea

HITTITES

HURRIANS

ASSYRIA

Nineveh

Ecbatana

Haran

Aleppo

Euphrates R.

Tigris R.

KITTIM
(CYPRUS)

Ugarit
Hamath

M E S O P O T A M I A

Asshur

Mediterranean Sea

Gebal (Byblos)

Sidon
Tyre
Dor
Gaza
Beersheba

S Y R I A

Damascus

Mari

B A B Y L O N I A

Susa

Hazor
Shechem
Jerusalem
Hebron

C A N A A N

Babylon

S U M E R

→ Route of Abraham

Areas under the influence of key
ancient powers (c. 1350 B.C.)

Egypt

Hittite Empire

Babylonian Empire

LIBYA

Dead Sea

ARABIAN DESERT

Ur

Persian
Gulf

0   125   250   500

Kilometers

© 2006, United Bible Societies

EGYPT

Nile R.

MIDIÁN

Red Sea

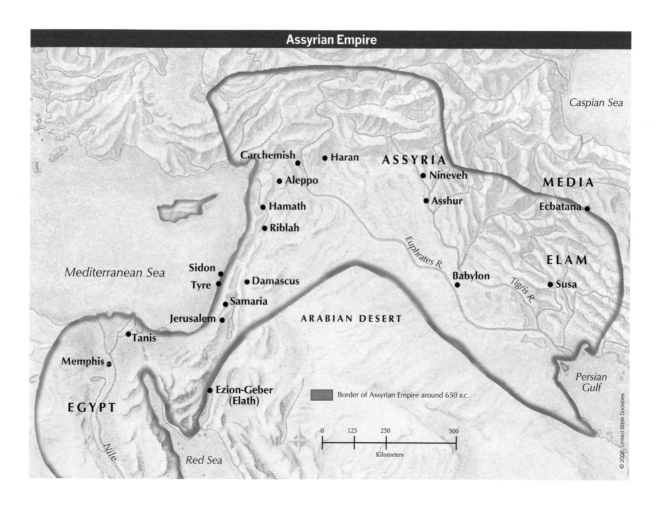

Assyrian Empire

Caspian Sea

Carchemish • Haran
ASSYRIA
• Aleppo • Nineveh
MEDIA
• Hamath • Asshur
Ecbatana •
• Riblah

Mediterranean Sea
ELAM
Sidon •
Euphrates R.
Tyre • • Damascus Babylon • • Susa
• Samaria Tigris R.
Jerusalem • ARABIAN DESERT

• Tanis

Memphis •
Persian
Gulf

EGYPT
Ezion-Geber
(Elath) • ▬ Border of Assyrian Empire around 650 B.C.

Nile
0   125   250   500

Red Sea Kilometers

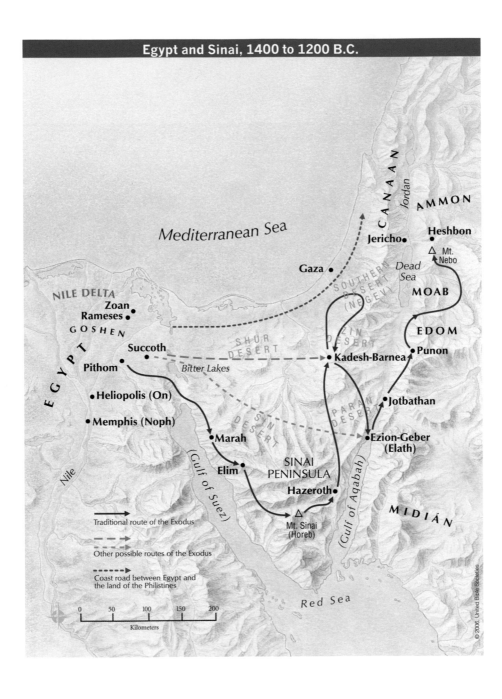

Egypt and Sinai, 1400 to 1200 B.C.

Mediterranean Sea

NILE DELTA
Zoan
Rameses
G O S H E N
EGYPT
Pithom
Heliopolis (On)
Memphis (Noph)
Nile
Succoth
Bitter Lakes
SHUR DESERT
DESERT
Marah
Elim
(Gulf of Suez)
SINAI PENINSULA
Hazeroth
Mt. Sinai (Horeb)

CANAAN
Jordan
AMMON
Heshbon
Jericho
Mt. Nebo
Gaza
Dead Sea
SOUTHERN DESERT (NEGEV)
MOAB
ZIN DESERT
Kadesh-Barnea
EDOM
Punon
PARAN DESERT
Jotbathan
Ezion-Geber (Elath)
(Gulf of Aqabah)
MIDIÁN
Red Sea

Traditional route of the Exodus

Other possible routes of the Exodus

Coast road between Egypt and the land of the Philistines

0   50   100   150   200
Kilometers

© 2006, United Bible Societies

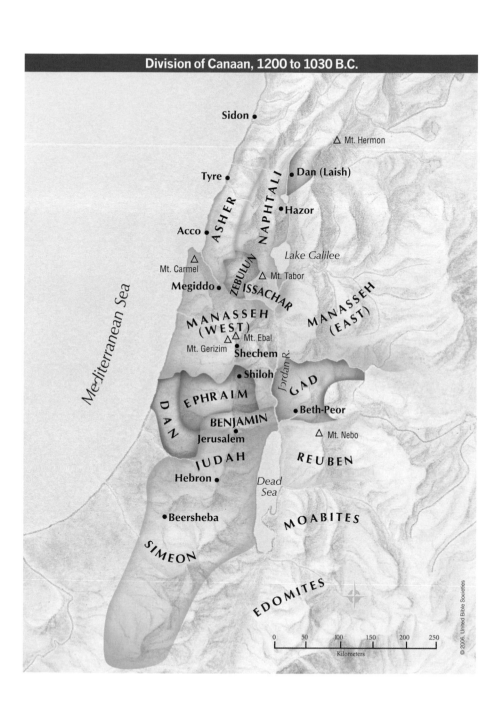

Division of Canaan, 1200 to 1030 B.C.

Sidon

△ Mt. Hermon

Tyre

Dan (Laish)

ASHER

NAPHTALI

Hazor

Acco

Lake Galilee

△ Mt. Carmel

ZEBULUN

△ Mt. Tabor

Megiddo

ISSACHAR

Mediterranean Sea

MANASSEH (WEST)

MANASSEH (EAST)

△△ Mt. Ebal

Mt. Gerizim

Shechem

Jordan R.

Shiloh

GAD

DAN

EPHRAIM

Beth-Peor

BENJAMIN

△ Mt. Nebo

Jerusalem

JUDAH

REUBEN

Hebron

Dead Sea

Beersheba

MOABITES

SIMEON

EDOMITES

0   50   100   150   200   250
Kilometers

© 2006 United Bible Societies

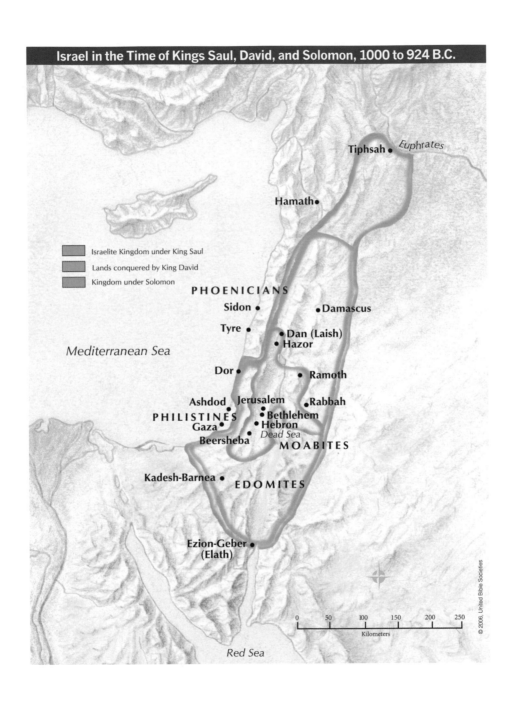

Israel in the Time of Kings Saul, David, and Solomon, 1000 to 924 B.C.

Tiphsah •

Euphrates

Hamath •

Israelite Kingdom under King Saul

Lands conquered by King David

Kingdom under Solomon

PHOENICIANS

Sidon •

• Damascus

Tyre •

• Dan (Laish)
• Hazor

Mediterranean Sea

Dor •

• Ramoth

Ashdod • Jerusalem

• Rabbah

PHILISTINES
Gaza •

• Bethlehem
• Hebron

Beersheba •

Dead Sea

MOABITES

Kadesh-Barnea •   **EDOMITES**

Ezion-Geber •
(Elath)

0   50   100   150   200   250
Kilometers

Red Sea

© 2006, United Bible Societies

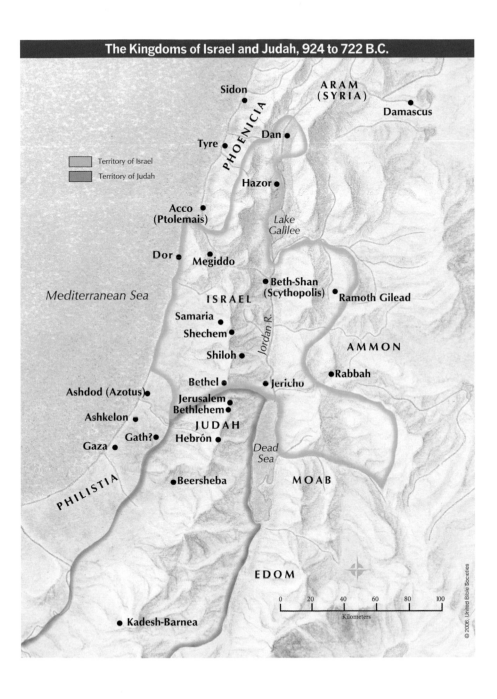

The Kingdoms of Israel and Judah, 924 to 722 B.C.

ARAM (SYRIA)

Sidon

Damascus

PHOENICIA

Tyre

Dan

Hazor

Territory of Israel

Territory of Judah

Acco (Ptolemais)

Lake Galilee

Dor

Megiddo

Beth-Shan (Scythopolis)

Ramoth Gilead

Mediterranean Sea

ISRAEL

Samaria

Jordan R.

Shechem

AMMON

Shiloh

Rabbah

Bethel

Jericho

Ashdod (Azotus)

Jerusalem

Bethlehem

Ashkelon

JUDAH

Gath?

Hebrón

Dead Sea

Gaza

Beersheba

MOAB

PHILISTIA

EDOM

0   20   40   60   80   100
Kilometers

Kadesh-Barnea

© 2006 United Bible Societies

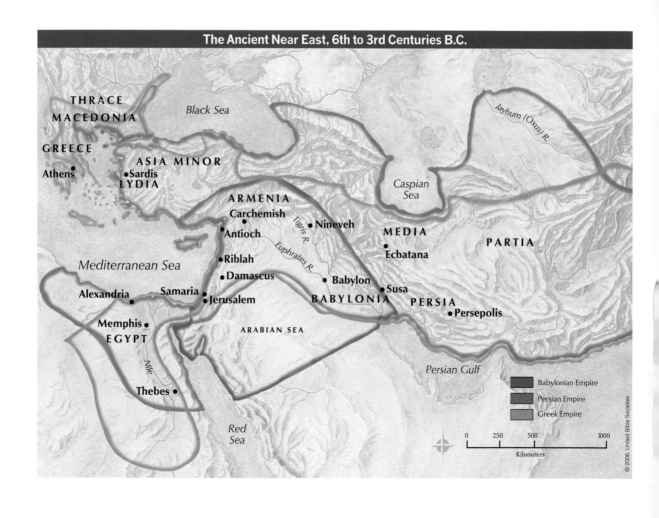

The Ancient Near East, 6th to 3rd Centuries B.C.

THRACE
MACEDONIA

Black Sea

GREECE

ASIA MINOR

Athens •

• Sardis
LYDIA

Jayhum (Oxus) R.

ARMENIA

Carchemish •

• Nineveh

Caspian Sea

• Antioch

Tigris R.

MEDIA

PARTIA

Mediterranean Sea

• Riblah

Euphrates R.

• Ecbatana

• Damascus

Alexandria •

Samaria •

• Babylon

• Jerusalem

• Susa

BABYLONIA

PERSIA

Memphis •

ARABIAN SEA

• Persepolis

EGYPT

Nile

Persian Gulf

Thebes •

Babylonian Empire

Persian Empire

Greek Empire

Red Sea

0   250   500   1000

Kilometers

© 2006. United Bible Societies

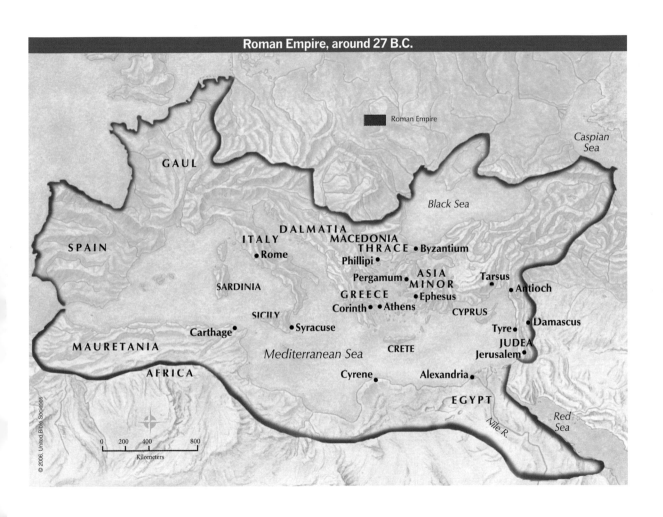

Roman Empire, around 27 B.C.

Roman Empire

GAUL

SPAIN

Caspian Sea

Black Sea

DALMATIA

ITALY
• Rome

MACEDONIA

THRACE • Byzantium

Phillipi •

SARDINIA

Pergamum •

ASIA MINOR

Tarsus •

• Antioch

GREECE • Ephesus

Corinth • • Athens

CYPRUS

• Damascus

SICILY

Tyre •

Carthage •

• Syracuse

JUDEA

Jerusalem •

MAURETANIA

Mediterranean Sea

CRETE

AFRICA

Cyrene •

Alexandria •

EGYPT

Nile R.

Red Sea

0   200   400   800
Kilometers

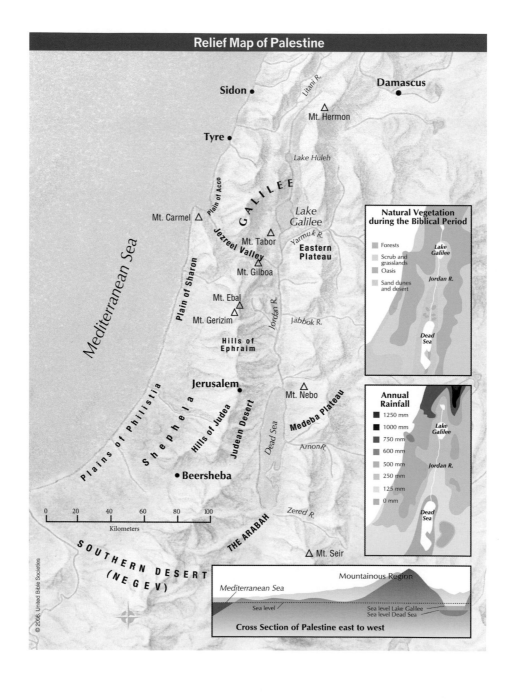

Relief Map of Palestine

Sidon •

Litani R.

Damascus •

△ Mt. Hermon

Tyre •

Lake Huleh

Plain of Acco

G A L I L E E

Mt. Carmel △

Lake Galilee

Jezreel Valley

Mt. Tabor △

Yarmuk R.

Eastern Plateau

Mt. Gilboa △

Plain of Sharon

Mt. Ebal △
△
Mt. Gerizim

Jordan R.

Jabbok R.

Hills of Ephraim

Mediterranean Sea

Jerusalem •

Mt. Nebo △

Medeba Plateau

Plains of Philistia

Shephela

Hills of Judea

Judean Desert

Dead Sea

Arnon R.

• **Beersheba**

| 0 | 20 | 40 | 60 | 80 | 100 |

Kilometers

Zered R.

THE ARABAH

**S O U T H E R N   D E S E R T
(N E G E V)**

△ Mt. Seir

Natural Vegetation during the Biblical Period

- Forests
- Scrub and grasslands
- Oasis
- Sand dunes and desert

Lake Galilee

Jordan R.

Dead Sea

Annual Rainfall

- 1250 mm
- 1000 mm
- 750 mm
- 600 mm
- 500 mm
- 250 mm
- 125 mm
- 0 mm

Lake Galilee

Jordan R.

Dead Sea

Mountainous Region

Mediterranean Sea

Sea level

Sea level Lake Galilee
Sea level Dead Sea

Cross Section of Palestine east to west

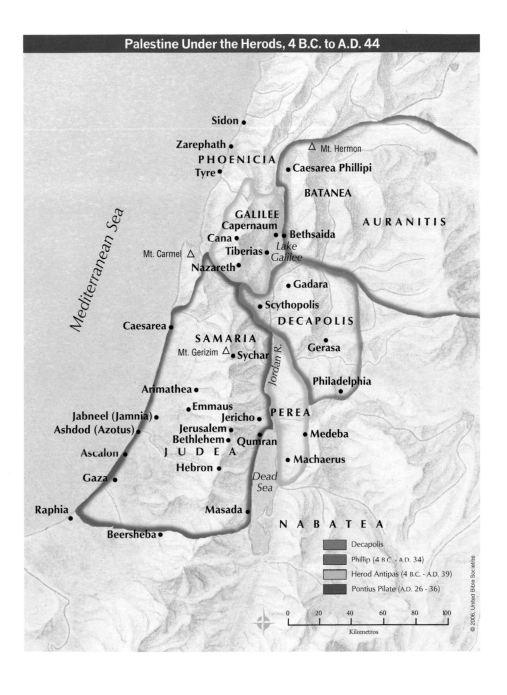

Palestine Under the Herods, 4 B.C. to A.D. 44

Mediterranean Sea

Sidon

Zarephath

PHOENICIA
Tyre

△ Mt. Hermon

Caesarea Phillipi

BATANEA

AURANITIS

GALILEE
Capernaum
Cana   Bethsaida
Tiberias   Lake
Galilee
Mt. Carmel △
Nazareth

Gadara

Scythopolis

DECAPOLIS

Caesarea

SAMARIA
Mt. Gerizim △ Sychar

Gerasa

Jordan R.

Philadelphia

Arimathea

Emmaus
Jabneel (Jamnia)   Jericho
Ashdod (Azotus)   Jerusalem
Bethlehem   Qumran
Ascalon   JUDEA
Hebron

PEREA

Medeba

Machaerus

Gaza

Raphia

Dead
Sea

Masada

NABATEA

Beersheba

Decapolis
Phillip (4 B.C. - A.D. 34)
Herod Antipas (4 B.C. - A.D. 39)
Pontius Pilate (A.D. 26 - 36)

© 2006, United Bible Societies

0   20   40   60   80   100

Kilometros

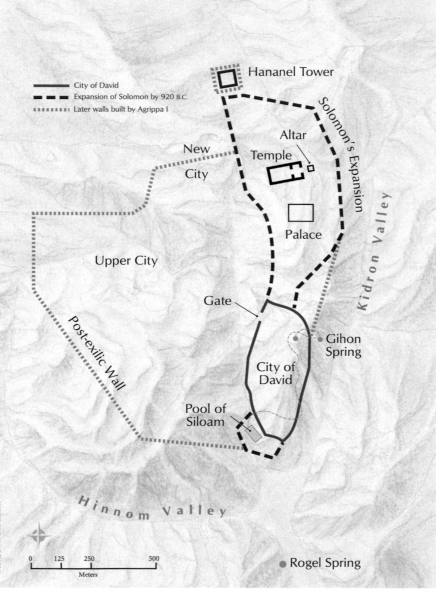

Jerusalem in Old Testament Times, 960 to 44 B.C.

City of David
Expansion of Solomon by 920 B.C.
Later walls built by Agrippa I

Hananel Tower

New
City

Altar

Temple

Solomon's Expansion

Palace

Upper City

Kidron Valley

Gate

Gihon
Spring

Post-exilic Wall

City of
David

Pool of
Siloam

Hinnom Valley

© 2006, United Bible Societies

0   125   250   500
Meters

Rogel Spring

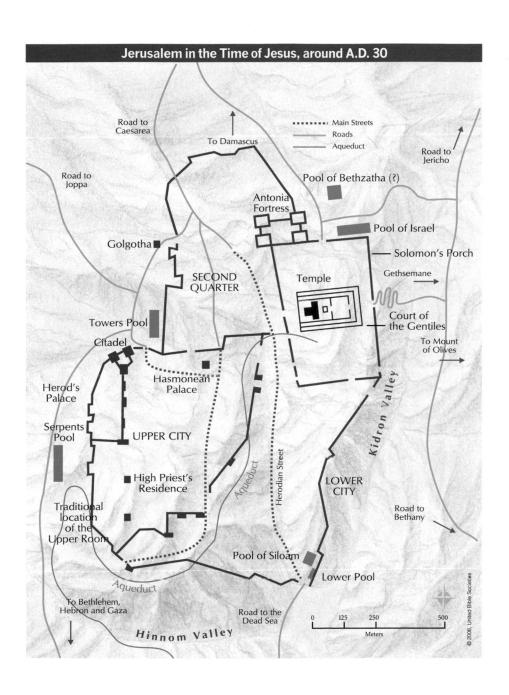

Jerusalem in the Time of Jesus, around A.D. 30

Road to Caesarea

To Damascus

Road to Jericho

Road to Joppa

Main Streets
Roads
Aqueduct

Pool of Bethzatha (?)

Antonia Fortress

Pool of Israel

Golgotha

Solomon's Porch

SECOND QUARTER

Temple

Gethsemane

Towers Pool

Court of the Gentiles

Citadel

To Mount of Olives

Herod's Palace

Hasmonean Palace

Kidron Valley

Serpents Pool

UPPER CITY

High Priest's Residence

LOWER CITY

Aqueduct

Herodian Street

Road to Bethany

Traditional location of the Upper Room

Pool of Siloam

Lower Pool

To Bethlehem, Hebron and Gaza

Aqueduct

Road to the Dead Sea

0   125   250   500
Meters

Hinnom Valley

© 2006, United Bible Societies

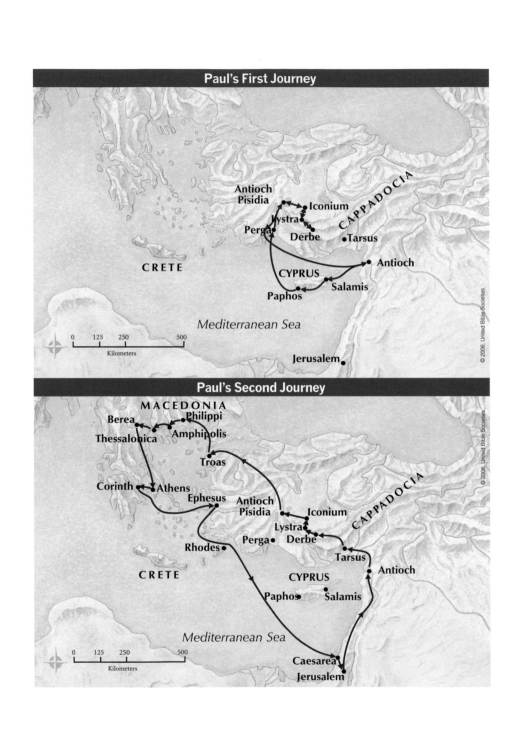

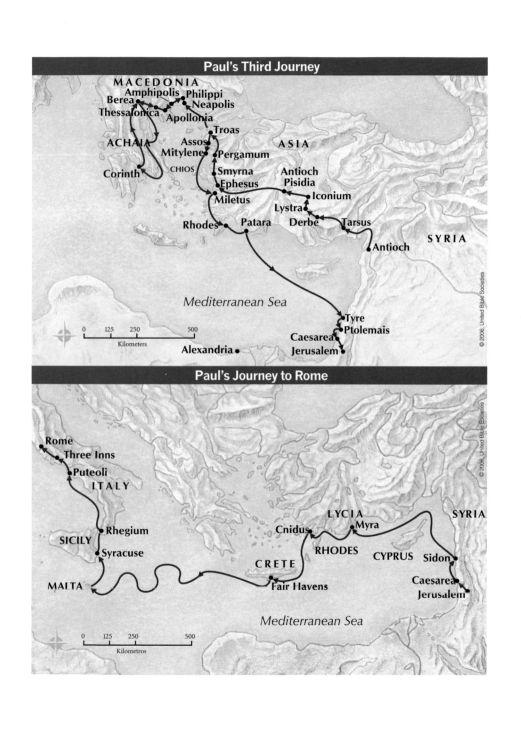

Paul's Third Journey

MACEDONIA
Amphipolis
Berea
Thessalonica
Apollonia
Philippi
Neapolis
Troas
ACHAIA
Assos
Mitylene
Pergamum
ASIA
Corinth
CHIOS
Smyrna
Ephesus
Miletus
Antioch Pisidia
Iconium
Lystra
Rhodes
Patara
Derbe
Tarsus
Antioch
SYRIA

Mediterranean Sea

0   125   250   500
Kilometers

Tyre
Ptolemais
Caesarea
Jerusalem
Alexandria

Paul's Journey to Rome

Rome
Three Inns
Puteoli
ITALY
Rhegium
SICILY
Syracuse
MALTA
LYCIA
Cnidus
Myra
SYRIA
RHODES
CRETE
CYPRUS
Sidon
Fair Havens
Caesarea
Jerusalem

Mediterranean Sea

0   125   250   500
Kilometros

© 2006, United Bible Societies

NOTES

EVERY DAY IS A JOURNEY.
GET SOME DIRECTION.

A new beginning // A disaster // A turning point
Same old same old // Something amazing
Something awful // Exactly what you thought
Something you never ever expected

Discover hope, encouragement and direction offered in God's Word through the ancient Catholic method of *Lectio Divina*, a prayerful approach to reading Scripture. Using the USCCB's Roman Catholic lectionary calendar, prepare for liturgy of the Word on a weekly basis.

Visit **ABSJourneys.org** today.

AMERICAN BIBLE SOCIETY

JOURNEYS
something good every day

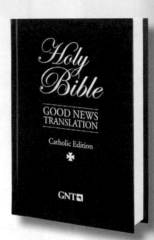
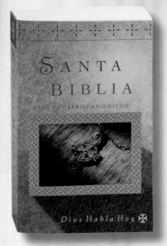